Some
of my
best
friends
are
Cookies

Over 80 recipes for the best cookies of your life

Some of my best friends are Cookies

Emelia Jackson

murdoch books

Sydney | London

For my littlest cookie, Mac. Oh, how I can't wait to bake cookies
with you and your sister, my beautiful boy.

And for my baba, Fani, one of the great loves of my life.
She was pretty partial to a cookie, my wonderful bubs.

Contents.

Introduction —— 9

Let's talk about cookies. —— 10

How to get your cookies perfectly round. —— 12

Ingredients I LOVE. —— 15

Tools of the trade. —— 18

Baking and storing your cookies. —— 21

The Basic B*kkies —— 23

The Quirky Cookie —— 77

The Classy Gal —— 133

The World Traveller —— 185

Acknowledgements. —— 226

Index. —— 228

Introduction

When writing my first book, *First, Cream the Butter and Sugar*, I well and truly went down the cookie wormhole. I dove headfirst into enthusiastically researching all of the cookie possibilities out there. So much so, that I lost track of time, missed my personally set deadline of when I needed to finish the chapter and caused myself a small amount of stress wondering if I was ever going to get the book completed.

I lost myself to cookies. I was drawn in, somewhat obsessively, to the world of cookies and the more I researched, the more I found. And the more I found? The more recipes I wanted to include in the book. My appreciation for cookies grew enormously during that time. Don't get me wrong, I've always loved cookies; I'm a baker and an absolute sugar fiend, after all. However, I came to see cookies as much more than just a simple and quick bake that was designed to satisfy a craving.

Cookies require a broad skill set and bucketloads of patience, and they're laced with cultural and historical significance. Recipes have been passed down from generation to generation, honouring their origins while exploring the possibilities of more readily available ingredients we have access to now. Cookies have a unique way of pulling you into blissful childhood memories – didn't everyone grow up with a maroon-lidded Tupperware container of biscuits lurking in the back of the pantry? (Or perhaps this memory is unique to the Jackson clan.)

For me, there is something very alluring about cookies. Is it discovering that baking cookies requires much more skill and patience than I originally thought, yet retains the fun and instant gratification of the most simple of bakes? Is it that you can take a few basic ingredients, along with an hour or two of your time, and create something so universally loved? Maybe it's just that butter and sugar, in all of their glorious forms, make up a vast amount of my DNA.

This cookie companion honours the classics we all know and love, while challenging the status quo with new flavour combinations and textural surprises that will have you thinking differently about what it is that makes a cookie (hello, Sticky date whoopie pies, page 129). The classics are embraced, new and exciting ingredients are introduced, and the humble cookie is advanced to new heights to take its rightful place amongst the best of bakes.

Let's talk about cookies.

... and biscuits. Now, before all of you come at me, I am well aware that the term cookie is very much an American one and that I am an Australian writer. However, I think there's a distinct difference between cookies and what the British and we Australians call biscuits. A cookie, in my opinion, is soft and chewy, and spreads when baked. A biscuit, on the other hand, snaps, and tends to be a little more brittle, sometimes sandy, and delightfully crunchy. Chocolate chip? A cookie. Scottish shortbread? A biscuit. Different. Both amazing.

But let's not get hung up on names (a rose by any other name and all that). Bottom line? Some of my best friends are cookies and some of them are biscuits. And you'll find them all hanging out together in this book. They're getting along just fine.

There are several types of cookie and biscuit doughs.

1. **Bar cookies**

Bar cookies are, as the name suggests, made from a dough that is baked in a tin and then sliced into bars. Examples in this book include Triple-chocolate cookie bars (page 62), Lemon, lime and bitters bars (page 130) and Earl Grey millionaire shortbread (page 143). Essentially, most recipes could become a bar cookie – press my chocolate-chip cookie batter (page 30) into a tin and... bam! You now have a bar cookie.

2. **Drop cookies**

Drop cookies are made with a soft dough that is spooned onto a tray before baking. They spread while cooking (so always leave plenty of room on the tray) and usually have a beautiful crisp edge and chewy centre. Everyone's favourite drop cookie comes to mind: chocolate chip (page 30). Others include Anzac biscuits (page 52) and The peanut butter cookie that almost wasn't (page 40).

3. **Filled or sandwich cookies**

Another one with a clue in the name, these cookies are filled or sandwiched with a ganache, jam, curd or buttercream. They are generally made from a rolled dough, but the term can be really used to describe any cookie that's sandwiched with a filling. Examples include Raspberry white chocolate melting moments (page 51), Chocolate hazelnut sandwiches (page 64) and Spiced plum and hazelnut Linzer cookies (page 188).

4. **Rolled cookies**

These are cookies that are made with a pliable dough that is rolled and then cut into shape. Generally, the dough has to be refrigerated before rolling, to firm it up and prevent spreading during baking. A few notable examples from the upcoming pages: Sables Korova (page 70), Chai-spiced sugar cookies (page 176) or Hazelnut praline squiggles (page 116).

5. **Moulded and pressed cookies**

Moulded cookies are made by moulding dough into a ball and pressing it into shape. Examples include Jammy thumbprints (page 46) or Passionfruit curd macadamia thumbprints (page 150). Pressed cookies are similar, but they're usually pressed through either a specialised tool or a piping bag fitted with a decorative nozzle, such as Viennese whirls (page 68) or Vaniljekranse (page 224).

6. **No-bake cookies**

If I'm totally honest, I don't really consider these to be cookies. But here we are. As the name suggests, these are 'cookies' that have not been baked, such as Almond and coconut chocolate clusters (page 180) and Almond toffee bark (page 222). Erring on the side of confectionery, I know.

How to get your cookies perfectly round.

Two things I absolutely must have in my cookbooks: a picture of every recipe (nobody wants to bake without knowing what the end result looks like); and enough instruction to ensure you will get similar results, without an overwhelming amount of additional information. As this is a cookie book, this page is a must read.

Cookies and biscuits, by their very nature of being sugar-and-fat-laden bakes (aka, perfection), are prone to spreading. They do their own thing in the oven. What enters the oven as a perfectly weighed out, rolled ball of dough will no doubt come out of the oven as a spread, lopsided and flattened cookie. While still delicious and perfect in its own way, it may not live up to your expectations of the symmetrical, gloriously round and uniform bake you set out to achieve. This is primarily relevant for drop cookies (e.g. chocolate-chip cookies and Anzac biscuits).

So how exactly do you achieve the perfectly round cookie?

1. Remove the tray of cookies from the oven a couple of minutes before they've finished baking. You want them to still be soft to allow for some shaping action.

2. Take a cookie cutter, ring cutter or anything round that's slightly wider than your cookies. I have a pack of ring cutters that has about ten different sizes in it. I highly recommend buying one.

3. Place the cutter over one of the piping-hot cookies and move it around in a circular motion, shaping the cookie as you move the cutter. Watch as your cookie goes from a randomly spread shape to a perfect circle, right before your eyes!

4. Repeat with the remaining cookies, then return your cookies to the oven for the final couple of minutes of baking.

And here's another free tip: perfectly placed chocolate chips can be added on top of your cookies as soon as you pull them out of the oven. The chocolate chips will melt with the heat but still hold their form and reset as the cookies cool, without burning the chocolate. Simple and pretty as a picture.

Ingredients I LOVE.

Butter

Use the best-quality butter you can afford –
it really does make a big difference to the
flavour of your bakes, especially for a simple
recipe like Scottish shortbread (page 26).

I always use **unsalted butter** for baking.
It allows you to control the salt content so
you don't end up with overly salty cookies.

Sugars

You'll notice that quite a few of the recipes
call for both brown and caster (superfine)
sugars, and for good reason.

Sugar is about more than the obvious
sweetness it adds. It holds moisture (in the
same way that flour does), amplifies flavour
(in the same way that salt does), is pivotal
in creating the desired texture, and acts as
a preservative, extending the shelf life of
your bake.

I use **caster (superfine) sugar** most
frequently in my bakes. It's a fine-textured
white (granulated) sugar that dissolves
easily when mixed into butter and doughs.
Generally speaking, caster sugar creates a
crisper cookie – important for recipes like
Chocolate ripples (page 73), which are all
about that snappy texture.

Light brown sugar or **dark brown sugar** is
caster (superfine) sugar with molasses mixed
in. It adds a more complex, caramel flavour.
More importantly, brown sugar is acidic
and is best friends with bicarbonate of soda
(baking soda), and that's why you'll often find
them together in recipes. When combined,
they create carbon dioxide, which aids in the
rising process of the dough. This ultimately
leads to less spread, more chew and more
puff in your bake.

Icing (confectioners') sugar is white
(granulated) sugar that has been ground to
a very fine powder (it's sometimes known as
'powdered sugar'). A little confession: I hate
sifting icing sugar! As such, I always use icing
sugar mixture, which is pure icing sugar
mixed with anti-lumping ingredients, such
as cornflour (cornstarch). If you're a purist,
feel free to sift to your heart's content, but
it's safe to assume I am using icing sugar
mixture (even in my macarons).

Flour

Plain or **all-purpose flour** has a gluten
content of around 9 to 11 per cent. This is
the main flour I use in my cookies as it has
a neutral flavour.

Eggs

I always use free-range eggs in my cooking.
While they are more expensive than the
caged option, from an ethical standpoint,
they are non-negotiable. I always use **extra-
large eggs** when I'm baking, so when you
see '2 eggs', it's safe to assume they are
59 g (2 oz) extra-large eggs.

A 59 g egg consists of:

- 9 g shell
- 50 g whole egg, made up of 30 g egg white
  and 20 g egg yolk

Knowing this, you can adapt the recipes
to the eggs that you have – convert the egg
quantities into grams and adjust accordingly.
For example, 2 eggs equals 100 g (3½ oz).
This also helps if you are halving, doubling
or tripling a recipe.

Cream
Thickened cream (as it's known in Australia – whipping cream or heavy cream elsewhere), has a fat content of around 35 per cent. It's a good all-rounder for ganaches and parfaits.

Baking powder and bicarbonate of soda
Both baking powder and bicarbonate of soda (or baking soda) are leavening agents. Bicarbonate of soda is often used in recipes that contain an acid, such as citrus juice or brown sugar. Baking powder is commonly used in recipes without a souring agent and instead reacts and rises with the application of heat.

Salt
Salt is a flavour enhancer – it balances sweetness and amplifies the flavours in your bakes. I like to use a fine granular salt in my doughs and a flaked salt to garnish my cookies (love a salty pop!).

Nuts and nut meals
Using nuts in your baking adds so many things – roasty, toasty flavour; crunch; texture; and moisture. Nuts are a great staple to keep on hand for upping the ante in your baking.

Nuts and nut meals are best stored in the freezer to prevent them from oxidising and turning rancid (bitter). You can buy nuts pre-roasted if you're planning to use them straight away but, for storage reasons, I prefer to buy my nuts raw and roast them as needed.

Vanilla
I am a lover of all things vanilla (it's actually one of my favourite flavours – second to chocolate, of course!). You'll notice my recipes call for more vanilla than you might be used to using. Feel free to cut back if you're not a vanilla fiend like me. I always use either a **vanilla bean paste** – I love the seeds in my bakes – or a good-quality **vanilla extract**.

Cocoa
I like to use the darkest cocoa powder I can find, known as **Dutch cocoa powder**. It has been processed to reduce the cocoa's natural acidity, meaning that the baking powder has the chance to do its thing. Dutch-processed cocoa is often labelled as either **unsweetened cocoa powder** or **100% cocoa powder**.

Chocolate

I buy my chocolate in bulk from Callebaut because I like the size of the chips, and they melt easily and consistently. Plus, they have a great flavour and come in varying strengths of cocoa solids, which means I can customise each recipe.

I'm not completely against supermarket chocolate – there are some good options available, such as Lindt or Nestlé Plaistowe. My general tip for baking is to use a '70% cocoa' chocolate, which means it contains 70 per cent cocoa solids. Even if you don't love dark chocolate, all of the sugar and butter in bakes tend to hide the chocolate flavour if you go for a lower percentage.

I like to melt chocolate in the microwave by heating it on medium in 30-second intervals. Stir between each burst so as to avoid burning the chocolate.

To temper chocolate, I also use the microwave – it's by far the simplest method. Simply add half of the chocolate you want to temper to a microwave-safe bowl (a heat-resistant plastic is best as it doesn't hold too much heat), and microwave on medium heat in 30-second intervals until melted. Dip your finger in to make sure the chocolate hasn't overheated – it should be just melted and not too warm to touch. Add the remaining chocolate and stir constantly until completely melted. The tempered chocolate should have a high gloss to it. You can spread a little on a plate and allow it to sit for 3–7 minutes; if it becomes matt and sets in this time, it's tempered. If it remains tacky and liquid, you have most likely overheated the chocolate and simply melted it. To remedy this, simply stir more chocolate chips into the melted chocolate until smooth.

Citric acid

I love citric acid. It's pure sour and because it's a powder, it won't affect the consistency of your glazes and fillings. Sour is a really important element in sweet baking – it balances sweetness and also makes flavours pop. Grab a jar of citric acid and have a play, bearing in mind that a pinch of citric acid goes a long way.

Gelatine

I usually use **leaf gelatine**, also known as sheet gelatine, in my cooking. However, I understand that powdered gelatine is much more accessible and, frankly, gives a more reliable set for marshmallows, as in my Chocolate marshmallow kisses (page 84).

Tools of the trade.

Good-quality, heavy baking trays or baking sheets

Buy good-quality trays that won't warp over time (this is especially important for making macarons) and will carry heat, ensuring perfectly golden cookie bums, every time.

Silicone baking mats

I love using silicone baking equipment, especially mats in place of baking paper. Not only are they more sustainable, but they will conduct heat, leaving you with those perfectly baked cookie bottoms.

Cookie scoops

These are commonly used to scoop ice cream, but are much better used for evenly portioning your cookies. I have three sizes for small, medium and large cookies. You can also divide and weigh out your dough balls, but scoops make the process so much faster. Don't cheap out on the scoops – the dough for drop cookies can be somewhat firm (especially if refrigerated), so you'll need a good-quality scoop to do the job.

Cookie cutters

I have a serious addiction to these and have found myself buying many random cookie cutters online during middle-of-the-night baby feeds. Here are my essentials:

- Nested ring cutters – great for both cutting out your rolled cookies and also shaping your drop cookies into perfect rounds once baked (see page 12).

- Fluted, nested ring cutters – these are purely decorative, but the fluted edge makes rolled cookies look much fancier! You could also buy one 5–6 cm (2–2½ inch) cutter in place of the nested pack.

- Optional extras – a Christmas tree, star and heart will be well loved. And a gingerbread man, of course!

Rolling pin with measuring rings

I have a rolling pin with measuring rings – google exactly that! The rings twist onto the ends of your rolling pin to ensure that your rolled-out dough has a consistent thickness. They usually come in 3 mm (⅛ inch), 5 mm (¼ inch) and 10 mm (½ inch) heights so your rolled cookies will have a consistent thickness every time. The measuring rings are also great for pastry work and tarts.

Piping bags and nozzles

Piping bags are used for making piped (or pressed) cookies, such as Viennese whirls (page 68) or macarons (pages 154–163). They're also very useful for neatly filling your sandwich cookies.

I recommend good-quality sturdy disposable piping bags (I use biodegradable ones from Loyal) and a few key piping nozzles:

- Wilton #1M or #2D – star shapes that can also be used for piping rosettes.

- Wilton #8B – a corrugated French star tip, which will give beautiful swirls (also needed for piping eclairs, but we'll save that for another book!).

- A 1 cm (½ inch) round metal piping tip – I prefer metal as they are the most durable and give the cleanest finish. The 1 cm round tip is great for filling sandwich cookies, and also for piping evenly sized macarons and meringue kisses.

Scales and microscales

Measure everything. And then measure again. I couldn't live without my digital scales and my microscales (so handy for measuring tiny quantities with great accuracy).

Thermometer

Digital thermometers take the guesswork out of everything – Swiss meringue, Italian meringue, praline, candy making, custards and curds.

Food processor and mixer

I love my food processor. I use a Thermomix, but you can use something less fancy. Use it to crush hard ingredients, such as nuts, or cook your curds and Swiss meringue (for macarons, pages 154–163) to perfection.

I also highly recommend a handheld stick blender, such as a Bamix. They're great for emulsifying the glossiest ganache you've ever seen.

I suggest investing in a high-quality stand mixer. If you're going to buy a KitchenAid, I highly recommend the 4.8 litre heavy-duty machine, which has a strong motor and large bowl. I also love the Kenwood Chef XL – the accessories are flawless and it even has a folding function.

Microplane grater

A microplane is essential for zesting citrus fruits and grating spices.

Spatulas and scrapers

Offset spatulas are a must and probably the most-used piece of equipment in my kitchen. Spatulas are great for lifting your cookies off the baking trays; scrapers are great for cleaning benches and bowls.

Baking and storing your cookies.

Here's a final little flourish of information for you before you dive into the good bits – the recipes. I haven't added storage suggestions within the recipe pages, and that's intentional. How long you want to keep and eat your baked goodies is totally personal choice. I, for one, am all about minimising food waste, so things tend to live in my kitchen longer than some might deem acceptable.

However, with that said, cookies and biscuits are definitely at their best the day they are baked. I prefer to bake as many as needed and freeze the rest of the dough so that I have access to fresh cookies, on demand. To do this, I simply portion out my cookies into balls and freeze them in a tightly sealed plastic container. Dough balls will last in the freezer for up to 3 months. To bake, let the frozen dough thaw for 30–60 minutes and then bake as per the recipe instructions.

To store baked cookies, I recommend allowing them to cool completely before packing them away in an airtight container. This will help them maintain their freshness. Eat them within 3 days for the most amount of deliciousness. If you do feel like they are leaning towards the stale side, simply pop the baked cookies back into the oven at 180°C (350°F) fan-forced for 2–3 minutes to freshen them up.

Macarons (whether filled or just the shells) are best stored in the freezer and can remain frozen for up to 4 weeks before they begin to disintegrate. Pull them out of the freezer 30 minutes before you want to eat them, to give them a chance to thaw.

Finally, cookies that are completely coated in chocolate will tend to stay fresher for longer as they are naturally airtight.

All the recipes in this book are baked using the fan-forced function. When baking multiple trays at the same time, it's best to use the fan in order to circulate even and consistent heat. That said, you know your oven best. Play around with its functions and see what gives you the best results.

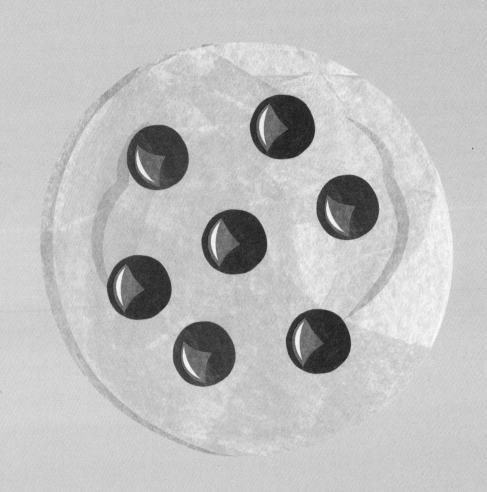

The
Basic
B*kkies

Scottish shortbread —— 26

The only chocolate-chip cookie recipe you'll ever need —— 30

Chewy ginger molasses cookies —— 34

Cocoa meringue kisses —— 36

Macaroons (not to be confused with macarons) —— 39

The peanut butter cookie that almost wasn't —— 40

Brown sugar and brown butter vanilla sables —— 43

Jammy thumbprints —— 46

Buckwheat chocolate brownie cookies —— 48

Raspberry white chocolate melting moments —— 51

Anzac biscuits —— 52

Lady fingers —— 56

Brown butter, spiced oat and chocolate-chip cookies —— 58

Sesame honey cookies —— 61

Triple-chocolate cookie bars —— 62

Chocolate hazelnut sandwiches —— 64

Lemon and poppy-seed crinkle cookies —— 67

Viennese whirls —— 68

Sables Korova —— 70

Chocolate ripples —— 73

Chocolate wheaties —— 74

Despite the name of this chapter, these cookies and biscuits are anything but boring. The haters keep saying that basic b*kkies aren't special enough, that they're generic and lack character. But, my friends, the opposite is true. These are the classics, the gold standard. Yes, the flavour profiles may not be wild and screaming 'Bake me! Bake me!' as you flick through the pages. But do you know what these b*kkies are? They're the white T-shirt and blue jeans of the baking world. They're not Gucci, and you're not wearing them to a wedding, but are they ever going out of style? I think not.

Think of your classics: chocolate chip, Anzacs, thumbprints, shortbreads – they're routine, but a must. Perfect for baking with your little ones, for the budding baker and for when you just want to enjoy the simple pleasures in life.

These are the comforting, simple and nostalgic sweety-treaties that I like to dip into my hot cup of tea during a rare moment of me-time on the couch. They're the cookies that will earn you comments like, 'Oh wow, my nan used to bake these for me, I haven't had them in years' or 'Good lord, I never knew peanut butter cookies could be that good' and 'Did you *really* bake these yourself?'.

Some of my favourite bakes are the basic ones. Now don't get me wrong, I love a multi-layered dessert project as much as the next home baker, but there is some real magic in mastering the basics.

JFK once said 'nothing compares to the simple pleasures of a bike ride'. I think that if you replace 'bike ride' with 'basic b*kkie and a cup of tea', I'm right there with him. Let's do this.

Scottish shortbread

Makes 14

This straightforward recipe is based on the general '1, 2, 3' ratio for shortbread: one part sugar, two parts butter, three parts flour. You can play around with the flour – plain flour, rice flour and cornflour (cornstarch) will all provide different textures (if you're adding rice flour or cornflour, you can expect a sandier texture). You can also add flavourings to up the ante; take a look opposite for inspiration.

This shortbread will forever remind me of my friend Jock Zonfrillo, a proud Scotsman who had a profound impact on the food industry and on my life.

180 g (6 oz) salted butter, softened
90 g (3¼ oz) caster (superfine) sugar, plus extra for dusting
270 g (9½ oz) plain (all-purpose) flour, plus extra for dusting

Using an electric mixer fitted with the paddle attachment, mix the butter and sugar until just combined and smooth, being sure to scrape down the side of the bowl. Add the flour and mix on low speed until the dough just comes together.

Wrap the dough in plastic wrap and refrigerate until completely chilled (1–2 hours or overnight). This will make the dough much easier to handle, while also reducing spreading during baking.

Preheat the oven to 130°C (250°F) fan-forced. Line a baking tray with baking paper or silicone baking mats.

Roll out the dough on a lightly floured bench into a 15 x 21 cm (6 x 8¼ inch) rectangle that's 1 cm (½ inch) thick. Cut the dough into 14 pieces, about 7 x 3 cm (2¾ x 1¼ inches), and place them on the baking tray. Use a fork to prick each piece of shortbread four times.

Bake the shortbread for 45–50 minutes or until pale blond but completely cooked through. While still hot from the oven, sprinkle the top with caster sugar. Allow the shortbread to cool for 10 minutes on the tray before transferring to a wire rack to cool completely before eating.

Pictured overleaf

Mix it up!

Chocolate-dipped coffee shortbread

Dissolve 1 tablespoon instant coffee powder in 2 teaspoons warm water to make a coffee extract. Add this extract to the butter and sugar mixture before beating. Once the shortbread has been baked and cooled, dip one side of each piece in 200 g (7 oz) melted milk chocolate.

Dark chocolate macadamia shortbread

Roughly chop 100 g (3½ oz) unsalted roasted macadamias and mix them through the finished dough. Roll the dough into a log and wrap in plastic wrap before chilling. Cut the chilled dough into 1.5 cm (⅝ inch) slices before baking. Drizzle the cooled shortbread with melted 70% dark chocolate.

Sour cherry and pistachio shortbread

Roughly chop 80 g (2¾ oz) roasted Iranian pistachios and 50 g (1¾ oz) dried sour cherries and mix them through the finished dough. Roll the dough into a log and wrap in plastic wrap before chilling. Cut the chilled dough into 1.5 cm (⅝ inch) slices before baking. Drizzle the cooled shortbread with a little tempered white chocolate (see page 17) and sprinkle with crushed pistachios before the chocolate sets.

The only chocolate-chip cookie recipe you'll ever need

Makes 20

If you recognise these beauties, you must be the proud owner of my first book, *First, Cream the Butter and Sugar*. When writing this cookie book, I was very conscious to not include recipes from my original tome... but with a name like this one, how could I not double up just this once?

These cookies are chewy and crisp, overloaded with chocolate and downright luxe. If you notice something different about it, it's that I've halved the recipe – the original makes 40 cookies, which is fairly indulgent, even for me.

Start these a day ahead to give the dough time to rest.

280 g (10 oz) plain (all-purpose) flour
½ teaspoon bicarbonate of soda (baking soda)
½ teaspoon baking powder
½ teaspoon sea salt flakes, plus extra for sprinkling (for that salty 'pop')
150 g (5½ oz) unsalted butter, softened
150 g (5½ oz) brown sugar
100 g (3½ oz) caster (superfine) sugar
1 egg, at room temperature
2 teaspoons vanilla bean paste
250 g (9 oz) dark chocolate chips

Combine the flour, bicarbonate of soda, baking powder and salt in a bowl. Give these dry ingredients a good whisk and set aside.

Using an electric mixer fitted with the paddle attachment, cream the butter, sugars, egg and vanilla. (I add the egg at this point because the added moisture helps the butter really cream up.)

Add all of the dry ingredients and the chocolate chips to the butter mixture and mix until just combined. Do not overmix the dough once the flour has been added – you don't want to develop any of the gluten in the flour, as this will leave you with a tough cookie.

This is the hardest step of all: refrigerate your cookie dough for 12–36 hours before baking. The longer you refrigerate the dough, the more flavour development will occur, the less the cookies will spread and the better the overall texture will be. Seems worth it, hey?

When you're ready to bake your cookies, preheat the oven to 180°C (350°F) fan-forced. Line two baking trays with baking paper or silicone baking mats. Place six golf ball-sized rounds of dough on each tray, using about 50 g (1¾ oz) dough for each one. The cookies will spread, so give them space to do their thing. Sprinkle with extra sea salt flakes.

Bake the cookies in batches for 12–14 minutes or until they're caramelised around the edges but still soft and blond towards the centre. To get your cookies perfectly round, see my tips on page 12.

Allow the cookies to cool on the trays for 15 minutes before transferring to a wire rack, then dive in, head first.

I always recommend eating the cookies with a cup of tea or coffee to ensure you can handle eating six in a sitting. We don't want that 'back of the throat' sugar build-up to hold you back from full enjoyment!

Note:
You can refrigerate the cookie dough for anywhere between 12 and 36 hours (or even longer if you wish, and you can even freeze the rolled dough balls). My general recommendation is 24 hours. If you just can't help yourself, you can bake a few cookies immediately and refrigerate the rest of the dough for the following day. Run your own experiments with timing and decide whether or not you think it makes a difference. The dough will be really firm once chilled, so you can roll the dough balls in advance and refrigerate them, ready to bake.

Pictured overleaf

Mix it up!
Leave out the dark chocolate chips and you have a great base recipe for any flavoured drop cookie. Here are some suggestions:

White chocolate, sour cherry and pistachio cookies
Add 175 g (6 oz) white chocolate chips, 60 g (2¼ oz) dried sour cherries and 60 g (2¼ oz) roasted pistachios.

Blueberry, lemon and white chocolate cookies
Add 200 g (7 oz) white chocolate chips, 30 g (1 oz) freeze-dried blueberries and the grated zest of 1 lemon.

Milk chocolate hazelnut crunch cookies
Add 175 g (6 oz) milk chocolate chips, 75 g (2½ oz) roughly chopped roasted hazelnuts and 25 g (1 oz) crispy dark chocolate pearls.

Hazelnut-stuffed chocolate-chip cookies
Refrigerate (or freeze) a jar of chocolate hazelnut spread (such as Nutella) or hazelnut praline paste for 30 minutes so it firms up. Flatten each ball of chocolate-chip dough into a disc and fill it with a heaped teaspoon of the firm chocolate spread or praline paste. Wrap the dough into a ball and make sure it's completely sealed before baking.

Raspberry and ruby chocolate cookies
Add 30 g (1 oz) freeze-dried raspberries and 175 g (6 oz) ruby chocolate chips.

Cereal chocolate-chip cookies
Keep the chocolate chips and add 90 g (3¼ oz) mini marshmallows and 30 g (1 oz) cornflakes.

Chewy ginger molasses cookies

Makes 20

These cookies are wildly American – not something we ever made growing up here in Australia. I have always been curious about them, though, drawn to the textures and flavours: warm spices, complex sugars and that alluring combination of chewy and crisp cookie.

They are a great cookie to sandwich with ice cream or parfait. I would stick to a basic vanilla ice cream here (not that anything about vanilla is basic!) to really allow the spices and molasses in the cookies to shine.

180 g (6 oz) unsalted butter, softened
110 g (3¾ oz) brown sugar
110 g (3¾ oz) caster (superfine) sugar
1 egg
70 g (2½ oz) molasses
330 g (11½ oz) plain (all-purpose) flour
1 teaspoon bicarbonate of soda (baking soda)
1 teaspoon salt
2½ teaspoons ground cinnamon
½ teaspoon ground nutmeg
½ teaspoon ground cloves
½ teaspoon ground ginger
100 g (3½ oz) demerara sugar

Preheat the oven to 170°C (325°F) fan-forced. Line two baking trays with baking paper or silicone baking mats.

Using an electric mixer fitted with the paddle attachment, cream the butter and brown and caster sugars until light and fluffy. Add the egg and molasses and mix to combine.

In a separate bowl, whisk the flour, bicarbonate of soda, salt and spices until combined. If your bicarbonate of soda is lumpy, you may need to add a sifting step here.

Add the dry ingredients to the butter mixture. Mix on low speed until just combined, ensuring you don't overwork the dough.

Roll the dough into 20 balls, using 40 g (1½ oz) dough for each one. Roll the balls in the demerara sugar before placing them on the baking trays, allowing room for spreading.

Bake the cookies for 14 minutes or until golden brown at the edges. They will appear quite soft, but will become chewy once they've cooled completely. Cool for 15 minutes to allow the cookies to set before diving in!

Hot tip:
Spray the bowl that you're measuring the molasses into with oil so that it glides right on out.

Mix it up!
To turn these molasses cookies into a crisp gingernut cookie, reduce the molasses to 40 g (1½ oz) and increase the ginger to 1½ teaspoons. Bake the cookies for 18 minutes to get a crisper, less chewy texture.

Cocoa meringue kisses

Makes 30
Gluten free

Are these cookies? I'm not entirely sure, but I tell you what: they're pretty, delicious, naturally gluten and dairy free, and I really wanted to include them here. Meringue-making is a core skill in baking, in my opinion, and these fancy little treats will become a staple in your cookie-baking repertoire. Plus, as a kid, those big, brightly coloured meringues in the bakery always seemed to call my name.

3 egg whites
¼ teaspoon cream of tartar
75 g (2½ oz) caster (superfine) sugar
75 g (2½ oz) icing (confectioners') sugar
250 g (9 oz) dark chocolate (70%), melted
30 g (1 oz) dark cocoa powder

Preheat the oven to 100°C (200°F) fan-forced.

Combine the egg whites and cream of tartar in the bowl of an electric mixer fitted with the whisk attachment. (The cream of tartar will help stabilise the meringue and reduce cracking.) Whisk on medium speed until soft peaks form. Slowly rain in the caster sugar, increase the speed to high and add the icing sugar. Continue whisking until stiff peaks form and you can no longer feel any sugar grains when you rub the meringue between your fingers.

Transfer the meringue to a piping bag fitted with a 1 cm (½ inch) star nozzle and pipe the kisses.

Bake the meringues for 1 hour, then turn off the oven and open the door slightly. Allow the meringues to cool completely in the oven.

Once cooled, dip the meringue bases in the melted chocolate, then dust them with the cocoa powder and allow to set.

Mix it up!
Leave out the cocoa for unflavoured meringue kisses, or replace it with 15 g (½ oz) of your favourite freeze-dried fruit powder for a fruity pop!

Macaroons (not to be confused with macarons)

Makes 18
Gluten free

Depending on where you land in Italy, you may have eaten these under several different names: macaroons, ricciarelli or amaretti. However (and please don't come for the jugular here), they are all very similar in that they are egg-white based, almond-meal-bolstered cookies that offer a dense, satisfying chewiness, with the bold sweetness of meringue.

You may notice that I haven't specified 'almond' in the recipe name and this is because I love to make these with different nuts, such as almonds, hazelnuts or pistachios. Simply replace the almond meal with your favourite nut meal. You can add the accompanying flavour extract to really go big on flavour.

250 g (9 oz) almond meal
130 g (4½ oz) caster
   (superfine) sugar
2 egg whites
1 teaspoon almond extract
   or amaretto
50 g (1¾ oz) glacé orange
   rind, diced (optional)
100 g (3½ oz) icing
   (confectioners') sugar
18 almonds (optional),
   to garnish

Preheat the oven to 140°C (275°F) fan-forced. Line two baking trays with baking paper or silicone baking mats. Combine the almond meal and caster sugar in a bowl and set aside.

In a separate bowl, whisk the egg whites until they begin to foam – you don't need to go for stiff peaks, but if you do, you'll end up with a beautiful rustic cracked cookie (which I love!).

Fold the almond meal mixture into the egg whites along with the almond extract or amaretto and glacé orange rind, if you're using it, and mix until you have a soft dough.

Roll the dough into balls, using 25 g (1 oz) for each one, and then roll them in the icing sugar before pressing an almond into the top of each (this is optional) and placing them on the baking trays.

Bake the macaroons for 15–18 minutes or until beginning to turn golden brown at the edges. Allow them to cool completely on the trays.

The peanut butter cookie that almost wasn't

Makes 15

I can't tell you how much trouble I had when developing this recipe. I tested, and tested, and tested again, but for the life of me, I could not get the texture I was looking for. I wanted the texture of a chocolate-chip cookie without the chocolate chips and, in their place, an intense peanut butter flavour. Test after test, I got cakey cookies. Or cookies without enough peanut butter flavour. Or cookies that spread to each end of the baking tray and burnt. Deflated and frustrated, I wrote down a new list of ingredients as a last-ditch effort to get these right, baked them off and... they were perfect. Perfectionists, rejoice!

Caveat: if you only have smooth peanut butter, use that, but the crunchy adds nice texture.

180 g (6 oz) unsalted butter, softened
150 g (5½ oz) brown sugar
100 g (3½ oz) caster (superfine) sugar
1 egg
250 g (9 oz) natural crunchy peanut butter (not the sweet stuff!)
100 g (3½ oz) plain (all-purpose) flour
½ teaspoon bicarbonate of soda (baking soda)
½ teaspoon baking powder
1 teaspoon sea salt flakes

Preheat the oven to 180°C (350°F) fan-forced. Line two baking trays with baking paper or silicone baking mats.

Using an electric mixer fitted with the paddle attachment, cream the butter, sugars, egg and peanut butter on medium speed until pale and fluffy, about 3–4 minutes. Mix in the flour, bicarbonate of soda, baking powder and salt. The dough will be super wet, but don't be tempted to add more flour – the peanut butter will undergo a transformation in the oven and behave much like almond meal does.

Using a cookie scoop or an ice-cream scoop, measure out 15 balls of dough, about 50 g (1¾ oz) each, and place them on the baking trays, leaving plenty of room for spreading.

Bake the cookies for 18 minutes or until golden brown at the edges. Leave to cool completely on the trays – these are quite high in sugar, so will be difficult to handle if you don't allow them to cool.

Brown sugar and brown butter vanilla sables

Makes 20

I love a simple biscuit; fewer ingredients often leads to subtle-yet-sophisticated flavours. The vanilla really shines here, which is why I've used the seeds of a whole pod (you can replace it with a teaspoon of vanilla bean paste or extract, though). These are understated, elegant and totally moreish.

The brown butter needs to be melted, then browned, and then reset. To make life easier, you can do this a few days ahead and store it in the fridge.

290 g (10¼ oz) unsalted butter
130 g (4½ oz) brown sugar
60 g (2¼ oz) icing (confectioners') sugar
2 egg yolks
270 g (9½ oz) plain (all-purpose) flour
½ teaspoon salt
1 vanilla bean, seeds scraped or 1 teaspoon vanilla bean paste
1 egg white, beaten
Demerara sugar, for rolling

Start by making the brown butter. Put the butter in a saucepan over medium heat. First the butter will melt, then sizzle, then it will foam and, finally, the milk solids within the butter will begin to brown. This enhances the flavour and adds a complex nuttiness that's beautiful in simple cookies like these sables. If you're unsure if you've browned your butter enough, you can weigh it – you should be left with 235 g (8½ oz) brown butter (the result of the excess water evaporating).

Transfer the brown butter to a bowl and place in the fridge to cool. This should take around 1 hour.

Put the cold butter in the bowl of an electric mixer fitted with the paddle attachment and add the brown sugar, icing sugar and egg yolks. Mix until just combined – you don't want to cream this mixture as it will result in the sables spreading. Mix in the flour, salt and vanilla.

Wrap the dough in plastic wrap and refrigerate for 1–2 hours to firm up.

Preheat the oven to 160°C (315°F) fan-forced. Line two baking trays with baking paper or silicone baking mats.

Roll out the chilled dough on a lightly floured bench until 1 cm (½ inch) thick. Use a ring cutter to cut out 6 cm (2½ inch) rounds and place them on the trays. (These rounds can be frozen if you don't want to bake all of the sables immediately.)

continued...

In a small bowl, whisk the egg white to break it down slightly. Put the demerara sugar in a separate bowl. Roll the outside edge of each dough round in the egg white and then gently press it into the sugar.

Bake the sables for 15–17 minutes or until lightly golden brown. Allow them to cool on the trays for 10 minutes before transferring to a wire rack to cool completely.

Mix it up!

You can turn these into plain vanilla sables by skipping the browning of the butter and using 225 g (8 oz) softened butter instead, and by also replacing the brown sugar with caster (superfine) sugar.

Jammy thumbprints

Makes 18

A thumbprint is a must here in the basic chapter. Not that it isn't glorious, I just think it's a biscuit that everyone who did some type of cooking class at school learned to make. We are zhooshing this one up a little by using a hazelnut biscuit base and a bright and tangy plum jam centre, with a pinch of citric acid added to amplify the sour notes. If these flavours don't float your boat, feel free to replace the hazelnut meal with the milder-flavoured almond meal and use any jam, ganache or curd of your choosing.

125 g (4½ oz) plain (all-purpose) flour
100 g (3½ oz) hazelnut meal
½ teaspoon salt
120 g (4¼ oz) unsalted butter, softened
60 g (2¼ oz) caster (superfine) sugar
Grated zest of 1 orange
1 teaspoon vanilla bean paste
100 g (3½ oz) good-quality plum jam
A good pinch of citric acid

Preheat the oven to 180°C (350°F) fan-forced. Line two baking trays with baking paper or silicone baking mats.

Put the flour, hazelnut meal and salt in a bowl and whisk to combine and break down any lumps.

Using an electric mixer fitted with the paddle attachment, mix the butter, sugar, orange zest and vanilla on medium speed until smooth, about 2–3 minutes. (You don't want to aerate the mixture, otherwise the cookies will spread.) Add the dry ingredients and mix until a soft dough forms.

Roll the dough into 16 balls, using 20–25 g (¾–1 oz) for each one. Place the balls on the trays, allowing room for spreading. Use the back of a teaspoon to press a divot in the centre of each ball.

Bake the cookies for 12–15 minutes or until lightly golden around the edges. Allow them to cool.

Combine the jam and citric acid in a small saucepan. Bring to the boil over medium heat, then cook for 2–3 minutes. Remove from the heat and fill the divot in each cookie with 1 teaspoon of the jam. (Heating the jam first will help it to set.) Let the jam cool completely before eating.

Buckwheat chocolate brownie cookies

Makes 12
Gluten free

These cookies are a riff on everyone's favourite – chocolate brownies – baked into cookie form. The method is almost identical to that of making brownies but instead of baking the batter in a slab and cutting it up, we use a cookie scoop or piping bag to form perfect little cracked rounds of brownie. When baked, they are chewy, fudgy, molten in the centre and magically crisp. They're perfect. Yes, perfect.

240 g (8½ oz) good-quality
   dark chocolate
   (minimum 60%)
40 g (1½ oz) unsalted
   butter
2 eggs
150 g (5½ oz) caster
   (superfine) sugar
30 g (1 oz) buckwheat flour
1 teaspoon salt
1 teaspoon vanilla extract

Preheat the oven to 200°C (400°F) fan-forced. Line two baking trays with baking paper or silicone baking mats.

Combine the chocolate and butter in a microwave-safe bowl and heat on medium in 60-second intervals, stirring in between, until completely melted. Set aside to cool completely.

Using an electric mixer fitted with the whisk attachment, beat the eggs and sugar until light and creamy. Fold in the cooled chocolate and butter mixture, along with the buckwheat flour, salt and vanilla.

Use a tablespoon to measure out the batter and place it on the baking trays, leaving plenty of room for spreading.

Bake the cookies for 10–13 minutes or until puffed up and cracked on the surface. Allow them to cool completely on the trays – if you move them while they're still warm, the bottoms can tear off.

Raspberry white chocolate melting moments

Makes 16

A nostalgic childhood classic, the melting moment is traditionally a custard-flavoured shortbread-style cookie that's sandwiched with vanilla buttercream (or passionfruit buttercream if you're feeling fancy). The world is your oyster in terms of flavours here; buttercream is easily flavoured with anything you love.

180 g (6 oz) unsalted butter, softened
70 g (2½ oz) icing (confectioners') sugar
200 g (7 oz) plain (all-purpose) flour
60 g (2¼ oz) custard powder

White chocolate raspberry buttercream
100 g (3½ oz) white chocolate, melted and cooled
85 g (3 oz) unsalted butter, softened
50 g (1¾ oz) icing (confectioners') sugar, sifted
1 tablespoon freeze-dried raspberry powder

Preheat the oven to 160°C (315°F) fan-forced. Line two baking trays with baking paper.

Using an electric mixer fitted with the paddle attachment, cream the butter and icing sugar until light and fluffy. Sift in the plain flour and custard powder. Mix until a soft dough forms.

Divide the dough into 32 evenly sized balls, using about 15 g (½ oz) for each one. Place the balls on the baking trays, leaving space for spreading, and gently press down with the back of a fork to form the classic indentations.

Bake the cookies for 15–18 minutes – they should appear to be dry and cooked through without becoming golden brown. Allow them to cool completely on the trays.

For the buttercream, combine all the ingredients in the bowl of an electric mixer fitted with the whisk attachment. Whisk on medium speed for 5–7 minutes or until the buttercream is light in colour and fluffy.

Sandwich the cookies in pairs, using about 1 teaspoon of the buttercream for each pair (or more if you're feeling it – I'm not about to censor your buttercream use). You can pop these in the fridge for 1–2 hours to set that buttercream before diving in.

Mix it up!

Nutella melting moments
Replace the custard powder in the cookies with 30 g (1 oz) dark cocoa powder. When making the buttercream, leave out the white chocolate and the raspberry powder, and add 100 g (3½ oz) chocolate hazelnut spread (such as Nutella).

Anzac biscuits

Makes 14

When I was writing *First, Cream the Butter and Sugar*, I remember having the distinct feeling that my cookie chapter was unfinished. I had gone a long way down the rabbit hole of cookie research and spent far too much time on the chapter, so decided that I needed to put it to bed and move on. It wasn't until the book was published that it finally hit me: I had written a modern Australian baking bible without including the most historically important biscuit for Australians, the Anzac biscuit. So here's to our Anzacs, my obsession with biscuits and cookies, and second chances in the form of single-topic baking books.

150 g (5½ oz) unsalted butter
100 g (3½ oz) golden syrup
150 g (5½ oz) brown sugar
½ teaspoon bicarbonate of soda (baking soda)
160 g (5½ oz) plain (all-purpose) flour
110 g (3¾ oz) rolled oats
80 g (2¾ oz) desiccated coconut
½ teaspoon salt

Preheat the oven to 160°C (315°F) fan-forced. Line two baking trays with baking paper or silicone baking mats.

Combine the butter, golden syrup and brown sugar in a saucepan over medium heat and bring to the boil. Remove from the heat and stir in the bicarbonate of soda (this will fizz!). Add the rest of the ingredients and stir until just combined – easy as that!

Roll the mixture into balls, using 50 g (1¾ oz) for each one, and place them on the trays, leaving plenty of room for spreading.

Now, here is the contentious question regarding the Anzac biscuit: chewy or crunchy? Traditionally, they were baked until crunchy for the soldiers, but I prefer mine to have a little chew to them. For a crunchy biscuit, bake them for 18–20 minutes; for a chewy biscuit, reduce the cooking time to 14 minutes. Allow them to cool completely on the trays before diving in.

Warning:
When I was testing these, my partner, Craig, commented that 'these aren't a biscuit, they're a full meal'. Feel free to reduce the size of them as you see fit (and be sure to reduce the cooking time as well).

Pictured overleaf

Mix it up!

Earl Grey Anzac ice-cream sandwiches

When I filmed MasterChef in 2014, a fellow contestant, Sean, made these in the house and the flavour combination was spot on! I'm conscious that most people won't own an ice-cream machine, so this recipe is a ridiculously easy no-churn one.

4 Earl Grey tea bags
250 ml (9 fl oz) boiling water
800 ml (28 fl oz) thickened (whipping) cream
400 g (14 oz) tin sweetened condensed milk

Steep the tea bags in the boiling water for 10 minutes or until concentrated and strong. Allow to cool. Whip the cream to stiff peaks, then fold in the condensed milk and tea. Pour the mixture into a 20 cm (8 inch) square baking dish lined with baking paper and freeze for 4–6 hours (or overnight). Once set, use a ring cutter to cut rounds of ice cream the same size as your Anzac biscuits. Sandwich each ice-cream round between two biscuits, wrap in plastic wrap and set in the freezer until ready to eat.

Lady fingers

Makes 20

These biscuits are ridiculously simply to make, with just five ingredients, and can be used to make everyone's favourite, tiramisu, or your Christmas trifle. Or just dunk them into your coffee. You can experiment here and replace some of the flour with cocoa or matcha, or try using brown sugar for a caramel twist on the classic.

2 eggs
85 g (3 oz) caster
    (superfine) sugar
100 g (3½ oz) plain
    (all-purpose) flour
¼ teaspoon baking
    powder
20 g (¾ oz) white
    (granulated) sugar,
    for sprinkling

Preheat the oven to 180°C (350°F) fan-forced. Line two baking trays with baking paper or silicone baking mats.

Using an electric mixer fitted with the whisk attachment, whisk the eggs and caster sugar on medium–high speed until the eggs have tripled in volume and are pale and fluffy, about 5–7 minutes. Sift the flour and baking powder over the egg mixture and gently fold through, trying to retain as much air as possible.

Transfer the batter to a piping bag fitted with a 1 cm (½ inch) round nozzle. Pipe 5 cm (2 inch) strips of the mixture onto the trays, leaving plenty of room for the biscuits to spread and rise. Sprinkle the white sugar over the biscuits.

Bake the biscuits for 10–12 minutes or until lightly golden brown. Allow them to cool completely on the trays.

Brown butter, spiced oat and chocolate-chip cookies

Makes 20

This is a beautiful, slightly more hearty/adult variation of the chocolate-chip cookie, and a must-include in my opinion. It's heavily spiced, which pairs perfectly with the dark chocolate, and is backed by the earthy tones of the rolled oats. You can prepare the brown butter a few days in advance and store it in the fridge.

290 g (10¼ oz) unsalted butter
180 g (6 oz) brown sugar
110 g (3¾ oz) caster (superfine) sugar
2 eggs
1 tablespoon vanilla extract
210 g (7½ oz) plain (all-purpose) flour
1 teaspoon bicarbonate of soda (baking soda)
1 teaspoon ground cinnamon
½ teaspoon ground nutmeg
½ teaspoon sea salt flakes
180 g (6 oz) rolled oats
200 g (7 oz) dark chocolate (70%), chopped, plus extra for sprinkling

Start by making the brown butter. Put the butter in a saucepan over medium heat. First the butter will melt, then sizzle, then it will foam and, finally, the milk solids within the butter will begin to brown. This enhances the flavour and adds a complex nuttiness. If you're unsure if you've browned your butter enough, weigh it – you should be left with 235 g (8½ oz) brown butter (the result of the excess water evaporating). Transfer the brown butter to a bowl and place in the fridge to cool. This should take around 1 hour.

Preheat the oven to 200°C (400°F) fan-forced. Line two baking trays with baking paper or silicone baking mats.

Using an electric mixer fitted with the paddle attachment, cream the brown butter and the brown and caster sugars until pale and creamy. Add the eggs and vanilla and mix to combine.

Add the flour, bicarbonate of soda, cinnamon, nutmeg and sea salt and gently mix until just combined. Add the rolled oats and chopped chocolate and mix until just combined.

Using a cookie scoop or an ice-cream scoop, scoop out even balls of the dough and place them on the baking trays, leaving plenty of room for spreading.

Bake the cookies for 12–15 minutes or until the edges are perfectly golden brown. Halfway through the baking time, shape the cookies into perfect rounds (see page 12) and return them to the oven. While still hot, sprinkle some additional chocolate over the cookies; it will melt and give picture-perfect results. Allow the cookies to cool completely on the trays.

Mix it up!

Turn this into my all-time favourite cookie – oat and raisin. Simply swap the chopped dark chocolate with 130 g (4½ oz) raisins or sultanas. Heaven.

Sesame honey cookies

Makes 32

The fun, floral aroma from the baked honey (which caramelises in the oven and transforms into something magical) with the nutty, almost savoury hum of the sesame tahini is a delightful combination. This is a simple drop cookie that's been amped up with some seriously moreish, adult flavours. These are great with a strong coffee, and also make the perfect vehicle for an ice-cream sandwich.

125 g (4½ oz) unsalted
   butter, softened
130 g (4½ oz) tahini
100 g (3½ oz) caster
   (superfine) sugar
100 g (3½ oz) honey
1 egg
160 g (5½ oz) plain
   (all-purpose) flour
¼ teaspoon bicarbonate
   of soda (baking soda)
½ teaspoon salt
Sesame seeds, for rolling

Preheat the oven to 180°C (350°F) fan-forced. Line two baking trays with baking paper or silicone baking mats.

Using an electric mixer fitted with the paddle attachment, cream the butter, tahini, sugar and honey until lightly aerated, around 2–3 minutes. Add the egg and mix to combine. Add the flour, bicarbonate of soda and salt and mix until just combined.

Put the sesame seeds in a bowl. Using a cookie scoop, scoop 20 g (¾ oz) balls of the mixture directly into the sesame seeds and roll to completely cover with the seeds. (This is more of a batter than a dough – the seeds add crunch and make the unbaked cookies easier to handle.) Place the balls on the baking trays, allowing plenty of room for spreading.

Bake the cookies for 14–15 minutes or until golden brown at the edges. Allow them to cool for 10 minutes on the trays before transferring to a wire rack to cool completely.

Triple-chocolate cookie bars

Makes 14

Introducing... the bar cookie! If you've read the introduction to this book, you will know that cookies are categorised into different types: drop, sandwich, rolled, moulded and this one, the bar cookie. This guy is in the basic section because I wanted to introduce the bar cookie to you with one element: no fillings, crumbles or icings, just the cookie bars. This recipe is completely customisable, and I've given a couple of examples of flavour combinations to get your creative juices flowing.

130 g (4½ oz) unsalted butter, softened
65 g (2¼ oz) brown sugar
90 g (3¼ oz) caster (superfine) sugar
1 egg
2 teaspoons vanilla bean paste
½ teaspoon salt
130 g (4½ oz) plain (all-purpose) flour
25 g (1 oz) dark cocoa powder
½ teaspoon baking powder
100 g (3½ oz) white chocolate chips
100 g (3½ oz) milk chocolate chips
50 g (1¾ oz) dark, milk and white chocolate chips, to garnish

Preheat the oven to 160°C (315°F) fan-forced. Line a 20 cm (8 inch) square cake tin with baking paper.

Using an electric mixer fitted with the paddle attachment, cream the butter, brown sugar, caster sugar and egg until creamy and pale in colour. Add the vanilla and salt and mix to combine. Make sure you scrape down the side of the bowl and the paddle to ensure there are no streaks of unmixed butter that will cause cracks in your cookie bars.

In a separate bowl, whisk the flour, cocoa and baking powder to combine. Add the dry ingredients to the butter mixture and mix on low speed until just combined. Add the white and milk chocolate chips and mix to combine.

Press the dough evenly into the tin and bake for 30–35 minutes (it will have puffed up slightly and appear dry on top). While the cookie slab is still warm from the oven, scatter the chocolate chips over the top. The residual warmth will slightly melt and secure the chocolate. Allow the slab to cool completely in the tin before slicing it into 3 x 9 cm (1¼ x 3½ inch) bars.

Mix it up!

You could bake pretty much any flavour into these bars, but here are some ideas to get you started.

Matcha, white chocolate and raspberry cookie bars

Replace the cocoa powder with matcha powder and the milk chocolate chips with extra white chocolate chips. Add 15 g (½ oz) freeze-dried raspberries or 90 g (3¼ oz) frozen raspberries.

Chocolate-chip and pretzel cookie bars

Leave out the cocoa powder and increase the flour to 165 g (5¾ oz). Replace the milk and white chocolate chips with 200 g (7 oz) dark chocolate chips, and add 100 g (3½ oz) crushed pretzels.

Chocolate hazelnut sandwiches

Makes 14

Now, before you all come for me and say these aren't basic b*kkies, let me tell you why they are (ish). Firstly, these bikkies are your introduction to the more complex/time-demanding/ suave bikkies you'll find in the next three chapters. They may look complicated, but really, all we're talking about here is a hazelnut shortbread, sandwiched with a simple milk chocolate ganache. The first step in this recipe is to roast and grind your hazelnuts. If this deters you from making these bikkies, simply use hazelnut meal instead. You won't get the same toasty notes, but you will save yourself a step, so there's that.

125 g (4½ oz) blanched
  hazelnuts
125 g (4½ oz) unsalted
  butter, softened
90 g (3¼ oz) brown sugar
1 teaspoon vanilla extract
170 g (5¾ oz) plain
  (all-purpose) flour
½ teaspoon salt

Chocolate ganache
200 g (7 oz) milk chocolate
100 ml (3½ fl oz) thickened
  (whipping) cream
¼ teaspoon salt
½ teaspoon vanilla bean
  paste

Preheat the oven to 160°C (315°F) fan-forced. Line two baking trays with baking paper or silicone baking mats.

Spread the hazelnuts over one of the baking trays and roast for 13–15 minutes or until golden brown and aromatic. Allow them to cool completely before transferring to a processor and grinding into hazelnut meal. Set aside.

Using an electric mixer fitted with the paddle attachment, mix the butter, brown sugar and vanilla until smooth. (You don't want to aerate this mixture, otherwise the cookies will spread.) Add the flour, salt and hazelnut meal and mix to a soft dough.

Roll out the dough until about 5 mm (¼ inch) thick. (This might seem quite thin, but will create a nice texture when the cookies are sandwiched together.) Cut out 6 cm (2½ inch) rounds (or any shape you like) and place them on the baking trays.

Bake the cookies for 12–14 minutes or until golden around the edges. Allow them to cool for 10 minutes on the trays before transferring to a wire rack to cool completely.

For the ganache, combine all the ingredients in a microwave-safe bowl and heat on medium–high in 30-second intervals, stirring in between, until completely melted. This should take 2–3 minutes in total. Allow the ganache to cool to room temperature, then transfer it to a piping bag fitted with a 1 cm (½ inch) corrugated star nozzle.

To assemble, pipe 1–2 teaspoons of the ganache into the centre of a cookie and sandwich it with a second cookie. Repeat with the remaining cookies. I like to pop these into the fridge for 30 minutes for the ganache to firm up before eating.

Lemon and poppy-seed crinkle cookies

Makes 35

Crinkle cookies aren't super popular here in Australia, but they should be. They are a pretty simple cookie dough that's rolled in icing sugar and granulated white sugar, giving a beautiful cracked appearance when baked. They're so good because they're light, zesty and fresh – not adjectives I've ever thought to use when it comes to cookies. I've added poppy seeds to these because why not?

125 g (4½ oz) unsalted
  butter, softened
210 g (7½ oz) caster
  (superfine) sugar
2 eggs
½ teaspoon lemon extract
Grated zest and juice
  of 2 lemons
350 g (12 oz) plain
  (all-purpose) flour
1½ teaspoons baking
  powder
30 g (1 oz) poppy seeds
80 g (2¾ oz) white
  (granulated) sugar
80 g (2¾ oz) icing
  (confectioners') sugar

Using an electric mixer fitted with the paddle attachment, cream the butter and caster sugar until light and fluffy, about 3–4 minutes. Add the eggs, lemon extract, lemon zest and lemon juice and mix until well combined. The mixture may look split at this stage due to the water content of the lemon juice; don't stress, it will come back together.

Add the flour, baking powder and poppy seeds and mix on low speed until the mixture just comes together as a soft dough. Here's the annoying part: this dough needs to be chilled to prevent the cookies from spreading too much in the oven. Chill it for 2 hours or even overnight.

After the dough has chilled, preheat the oven to 180°C (350°F) fan-forced. Line two baking trays with baking paper or silicone baking mats.

Put the white sugar and icing sugar in separate bowls. Divide the chilled dough into 25 g (1 oz) balls (using a small cookie scoop is the easiest way to do this). Roll the balls in the white sugar, followed by the icing sugar, then place them on the baking trays. (The two types of sugar are needed to create the crackled, almost candy-like end result.)

Bake the cookies for 13–15 minutes or until they have spread, crinkled and still appear slightly moist right in the centre (this will give you a fudge-like consistency). Allow them to cool for 10 minutes on the trays before transferring to a wire rack to cool completely.

Viennese whirls

Growing up, I really didn't like these biscuits. I didn't know why, but they never tasted quite right to me. I had one recently and I finally worked out what was so unappealing about them: they were dipped in waxy, overly sweet compound chocolate, which overwhelmed the entire experience. If you've only ever tried the mass-produced variety, you'll fall in love with these short, almost sandy cookies with the sophisticated subtlety of vanilla, dipped in a good-quality dark chocolate.

220 g (7¾ oz) unsalted butter, softened

90 g (3¼ oz) icing (confectioners') sugar

2 teaspoons vanilla bean paste

230 g (8 oz) plain (all-purpose) flour

30 g (1 oz) cornflour (cornstarch)

¼ teaspoon fine salt

Grated zest of 1 orange

1 teaspoon ground cardamom

150 g (5½ oz) dark chocolate, melted and cooled

100 g (3½ oz) pistachios, roasted and finely chopped

Preheat the oven to 180°C (350°F) fan-forced. Line two baking trays with baking paper or silicone baking mats.

Using an electric mixer fitted with the paddle attachment, cream the butter, icing sugar and vanilla until light and creamy, about 5–7 minutes. Scrape down the side of the bowl and paddle to make sure there are no unmixed lumps of butter remaining.

Sift the flour, cornflour and salt onto the butter mixture, and add the orange zest and cardamom. Mix on low speed until a smooth dough forms.

Transfer the dough to a piping bag fitted with a star nozzle and pipe the cookies into an 'S' shape onto the baking trays, around 3–4 cm (1¼–1½ inches) long. This will take some elbow grease as the dough is quite thick. Place the trays in the fridge for 30–40 minutes or until the dough is firm.

Bake the cookies for 15–18 minutes or until the edges are slightly golden. Allow them to cool before dipping each end of the cookies in the melted chocolate and sprinkling them with the chopped pistachios.

Mix it up!
Sandwiched with a beautiful raspberry jam, these are another level of good.

Sables Korova

Makes 16

These little round morsels of chocolatey goodness are also known as World Peace Cookies and are the brainchild of French pastry chef Pierre Hermé. They are bitter from the cocoa, with luscious pops of dark chocolate throughout, and should be just salty enough to leave you wanting more. These won't come together as a dough, so don't be tempted to add any liquid when mixing. The sandier the unbaked cookie, the better the final texture will be.

200 g (7 oz) plain
   (all-purpose) flour
45 g (1½ oz) dark cocoa
   powder
½ teaspoon bicarbonate
   of soda (baking soda)
120 g (4¼ oz) unsalted
   butter, softened
180 g (6 oz) brown sugar
½ teaspoon fine salt
1 teaspoon vanilla extract
150 g (5½ oz) dark
   chocolate chips

Combine the flour, cocoa and bicarbonate of soda in a bowl and whisk to break down any lumps.

Using an electric mixer fitted with the paddle attachment, mix the butter, brown sugar, salt and vanilla on medium–low speed until the mixture is softened and cohesive. Scrape down the side of the bowl to ensure all of the butter is incorporated.

Add the flour mixture and mix until just combined. The dough will look quite sandy at this stage. Add the chocolate chips and mix until the dough begins to clump. It won't form a cohesive ball – it will stay quite sandy, so don't stress!

Line your bench with plastic wrap and dump the sable mix in the centre. Press the dough together to form a log shape, then tightly roll it in the plastic wrap. You should have a 30 cm (12 inch) log, and you may need to wrap it a few times in extra plastic wrap to really get it tightly bonded together. Place the dough in the fridge for at least 2–4 hours (overnight is best). You can also keep the log in the freezer and bake the cookies directly from frozen.

Preheat the oven to 160°C (315°F) fan-forced. Line two baking trays with baking paper or silicone baking mats.

Slice the chilled dough into 1–1.5 cm (½–⅝ inch) slices. If they fall apart slightly, just press them back together – this is actually a good sign that you will get that nice sandy texture. Place the cookie rounds on the baking trays.

Bake the sables for 12–13 minutes or until they appear dry and set. Allow them to cool completely on the trays before attempting to move them.

Chocolate ripples

Makes 18

A chocolate ripple is an Australian biscuit icon and for one main reason: the chocolate ripple cake. If you don't know, you should. My US readers would call this an icebox cake. Basically, you layer the chocolate ripples with whipped vanilla cream, let it get all soft in the fridge overnight and then eat to your heart's content. Make these bikkies instead of buying them and live out your home-made chocolate ripple cake dreams.

150 g (5½ oz) unsalted
   butter, softened
250 g (9 oz) caster
   (superfine) sugar
90 g (3¼ oz) golden syrup
1 egg
200 g (7 oz) plain
   (all-purpose) flour
50 g (1¾ oz) dark cocoa
   powder
1 teaspoon bicarbonate
   of soda (baking soda)
¼ teaspoon baking
   powder
½ teaspoon salt
100 g (3½ oz) raw sugar

Preheat the oven to 160°C (315°F) fan-forced. Line two baking trays with baking paper or silicone baking mats.

Using an electric mixer fitted with the paddle attachment, mix the butter, caster sugar and golden syrup until just combined. Add the egg and mix to incorporate.

In a separate bowl, sift the flour, cocoa, bicarbonate of soda, baking powder and salt. Add the dry ingredients to the butter mixture and mix until just combined.

Roll the dough into 18 balls, using 40 g (1½ oz) for each one, then roll them in the raw sugar. Place the balls on the baking trays, leaving plenty of room for spreading.

Bake the biscuits for 18–20 minutes. Allow them to cool completely on the trays.

Chocolate wheaties

Makes 16

Another childhood classic bikkie, the chocolate wheatie (or digestive) is a sturdy biscuit with a healthy dose of wheatgerm, made all the better with a coating of dark or milk chocolate on the base (fork imprints are a must). As a kid, I actually loved these best a few days after the packet had been opened and the bikkie was a little soft with age. Wheatgerm can sometimes be tricky to find. Try a health-food shop, or replace it with rice bran or even roughly ground rolled oats.

110 g (3¾ oz) unsalted butter, softened
125 g (4½ oz) brown sugar
1 egg
25 g (1 oz) desiccated coconut
40 g (1½ oz) wheatgerm
160 g (5½ oz) wholemeal plain (all-purpose) flour
½ teaspoon baking powder
200 g (7 oz) dark chocolate, melted

Line two baking trays with baking paper or silicone baking mats.

Using an electric mixer fitted with the paddle attachment, mix the butter, brown sugar and egg on medium speed until just combined and smooth.

Add the coconut, wheatgerm, flour and baking powder and mix until a smooth dough forms.

Roll out the dough between two pieces of baking paper until 5 mm (¼ inch) thick. Use a ring cutter to cut out 7 cm (2¾ inch) rounds and place them on the trays. Chill the rounds for 30 minutes to prevent them from spreading during baking. (At this stage, you can freeze the dough rounds to bake at a later time.)

Meanwhile, preheat the oven to 160°C (315°F) fan-forced.

Transfer the chilled dough rounds onto the baking trays and bake for 18–20 minutes or until golden around the edges. Allow the cookies to cool for 10 minutes on the trays before transferring to a wire rack to cool completely.

Spread a generous amount of the melted chocolate over the base of each cookie. Use a fork to create grooves in the chocolate, then allow to set before eating.

The
Quirky
Cookie

Praline-stuffed chocolate-chip skillet cookie —— 80

Chunky Levain-style malted chocolate-chip cookies —— 82

Chocolate marshmallow kisses —— 84

Iced VoVo™ biscuits —— 88

Mint Slice™ biscuits, three ways —— 90

Apple pie cookies —— 94

Twixie Twix™ —— 97

Matcha, white chocolate and raspberry cookies —— 101

Pecan pie shortbread bars —— 102

Baklava cookies —— 104

Strawberry and cream bar cookies —— 108

Blueberry muffin top cookies —— 110

Cookimisu —— 113

Rhubarb lattice pie cookies —— 114

Hazelnut praline squiggles —— 116

Raspberry and white chocolate cornflake cookies —— 120

Blackberry cheesecake cookies —— 123

Raspberry rhubarb crumble bars —— 124

Pandan and coconut cookies —— 126

Sticky date whoopie pies —— 129

Lemon, lime and bitters bars —— 130

You've made it through the basics of chapter one, you're feeling a little more confident, a little more adventurous and, most importantly, a little more playful. Enter the quirky cookie. These recipes are certainly a level up in terms of preparation, flavours and, at times, ingredients. But with that next step comes a few of my favourite recipes in the book.

A little sneak peek: cookie skillets make an appearance and a few more Aussie icons show their faces. And while I had to test, then retest, then retest this one, I present to you the copycat Levain chocolate chunk cookie that actually works.

The quirky cookie is all things fun, flavoursome and frivolous; she is a touch more labour intensive than your basic b*kkie, but will leave you feeling like a biscuit-baking queen.

Praline-stuffed chocolate-chip skillet cookie

Serves 12

Even I will admit that this is pretty OTT, but it's my favourite way to transform the humble chocolate-chip cookie into a pretty luxurious and impressive dessert. It's best served warm with some vanilla ice cream.

150 g (5½ oz) hazelnut praline paste or chocolate hazelnut spread (such as Nutella)
200 g (7 oz) plain (all-purpose) flour
½ teaspoon bicarbonate of soda (baking soda)
½ teaspoon baking powder
½ teaspoon sea salt flakes, plus extra for sprinkling (for that salty 'pop')
130 g (4½ oz) unsalted butter, softened
110 g (3¾ oz) brown sugar
90 g (3¼ oz) caster (superfine) sugar
1 egg, at room temperature
2 teaspoons vanilla bean paste
270 g (9½ oz) dark chocolate chips
Vanilla ice cream, to serve

Preheat the oven to 180°C (350°F) fan-forced. Line the base of a 20 cm (8 inch) cast iron frying pan with a round of baking paper (the paper isn't essential, but it makes for an easier clean-up).

Spread the praline paste or chocolate hazelnut spread into a rough 15 cm (6 inch) round on a sheet of baking paper, then place in the freezer to firm up while you prepare the cookie dough.

Combine the flour, bicarbonate of soda, baking powder and salt in a bowl. Give these dry ingredients a good whisk and set aside.

Using an electric mixer fitted with the paddle attachment, cream the butter, brown and caster sugars, egg and vanilla. (I add the egg at this point because the added moisture helps the butter really cream up.) Add all of the dry ingredients along with 220 g (7¾ oz) of the chocolate chips and mix until just combined.

Press half of the dough into the base of the frying pan, pushing it out with your fingertips to the edges. Place the frozen disc of praline paste or chocolate spread in the centre of the dough. Press out the remaining half of the dough into a lid and place it on top of the disc. (As the cookie bakes, the dough will spread and seal, so don't be overly concerned about making it perfect.)

Bake the cookie for 35 minutes or until it's a beautiful golden brown. While the cookie is still warm from the oven, scatter the remaining chocolate chips over the top. Allow to cool for 10–15 minutes before slicing the cookie into wedges and serving it with ice cream.

Chunky Levain-style malted chocolate-chip cookies

Makes 13

I must be honest with you, I have never had a cookie from the famous Levain Bakery. While I absolutely adore New York and travelled there a few times in my twenties, my thirties have thus far been spent either in lockdown, writing cookbooks or having babies. As such, any frivolous opportunities to jet off to the great city on a whim have been totally non-existent. In any case, I have seen many influencers eating these cookies in such high resolution that, if I close my eyes tightly enough, I can just about taste them. The trick to mastering the thick cookie? Cold butter. We don't want this cookie spreading in the oven, and cold dough prevents that from happening.

125 g (4½ oz) unsalted
  butter, chilled
120 g (4¼ oz) brown sugar
75 g (2½ oz) caster
  (superfine) sugar
1 egg
1 teaspoon vanilla bean
  paste
280 g (10 oz) plain
  (all-purpose) flour
75 g (2½ oz) malted
  milk powder (such
  as Horlicks)
1 teaspoon salt
½ teaspoon baking
  powder
150 g (5½ oz) dark
  chocolate chips
175 g (6 oz) roasted
  hazelnuts, roughly
  chopped
50 g (1¾ oz) milk chocolate
  chips, to garnish

Preheat the oven to 160°C (315°F) fan-forced. Line two baking trays with baking paper or silicone baking mats.

Using an electric mixer fitted with the paddle attachment, mix the butter, brown sugar and caster sugar until just combined. (You don't want to aerate this mixture, otherwise the cookies will spread.) Mix in the egg and vanilla, followed by the flour, malted milk powder, salt and baking powder. Finally, mix in the dark chocolate chips and 125 g (4½ oz) of the hazelnuts.

Divide the dough into 13 balls, using 80 g (2¾ oz) dough for each one, and place them on the baking trays, leaving plenty of room for spreading.

Bake the cookies for 13–14 minutes or until golden brown around the edges. Scatter the milk chocolate chips and the remaining hazelnuts over the hot cookies. Allow them to cool completely on the trays.

Chocolate marshmallow kisses

Makes 10

If you grew up in Australia in the 90s, you'll know that these cookies were a god-tier level treat only brought out for the absolutely finest occasions. These require a little bit of prep time, along with a little bit of patience – there are a few steps! But they are oh so worth it. There's nothing quite as satisfying as watching the gelatinous concoction that is marshmallow whip up into silky, sticky clouds. Work quickly when piping, as the marshmallow will begin to set if you're not careful.

85 g (3 oz) unsalted butter
70 g (2½ oz) caster (superfine) sugar
1 egg yolk
1 teaspoon vanilla bean paste or extract
½ teaspoon sea salt
150 g (5½ oz) plain (all-purpose) flour, plus extra for dusting
250 g (9 oz) good-quality raspberry jam (or any jam you love)
250 g (9 oz) dark or milk chocolate, tempered (see page 17)

Vanilla marshmallow
400 g (14 oz) caster (superfine) sugar
30 g (1 oz) liquid glucose
1 tablespoon vanilla bean paste
14 g (½ oz) powdered gelatine

Using an electric mixer fitted with the paddle attachment, cream the butter and sugar until combined – you're not looking for this to be light and fluffy. Add the egg yolk, vanilla and salt and mix to combine. Add the flour and mix until completely incorporated.

Wrap the dough in plastic wrap and place in the fridge for at least 2 hours. (This will help reduce spreading during baking. You can make the dough the day prior and refrigerate it overnight, if preferred.)

Preheat the oven to 170°C (325°F) fan-forced. Line two baking trays with baking paper or silicone baking mats.

Roll out the chilled dough on a lightly floured bench until 6 mm (¼ inch) thick, stopping and rotating as you go to ensure it isn't sticking to the bench (and adding small amounts of flour if it is). Using a 5–6 cm (2–2½ inch) cutter, cut the dough into rounds and place them on the baking trays. (The dough rounds can be stored in the fridge until ready to bake and can also be frozen for later use.)

Bake the cookies for 12 minutes or until golden brown around the edges. If they spread in the oven, you can use your cookie cutter to cut them into uniform sizes again while still hot. Allow the cookies to cool completely on the trays.

Meanwhile, make the marshmallow. Combine 150 ml (5 fl oz) water with the sugar, glucose and vanilla in a saucepan. Bring the syrup to the boil and cook until it reaches 118–121°C (244–250°F) on a sugar thermometer (soft-ball stage).

While the syrup is cooking, combine 50 ml (1¾ fl oz) water with the gelatine in the bowl of your electric mixer fitted with the whisk attachment. Set aside to allow the gelatine to swell while the sugar syrup comes to temperature.

When the sugar syrup is ready, pour the syrup over the gelatine mixture and whisk on medium–high speed. As the gelatine cools, air will become trapped in the sugar syrup and the mixture will become pale and, for lack of a better word, marshmallowy. Transfer the marshmallow to a piping bag fitted with a round nozzle and get ready to begin assembling the cookies.

Take one of the cookies and spoon ½ teaspoon of jam onto the centre. Pipe the soft marshmallow over the jam to completely encase it, and pull the piping bag up to create a 'kiss' shape. Repeat with the remaining cookies. Allow the marshmallow to set for 20–30 minutes before dipping the entire cookie into the tempered chocolate. Place in the fridge for about an hour to allow the chocolate to set.

Pictured overleaf

Mix it up!

These can be flavoured in so many different ways – freeze-dried fruit powders, citrus zests or even flavouring extracts can be used in the marshmallow, different-flavoured jams can be used in the filling and different chocolates can all be utilised to create your own signature flavours.

Dulcey passionfruit kisses

Add 15 g (½ oz) freeze-dried passionfruit powder to the marshmallow while whisking, leave out the jam and dip the cookies into melted caramelised dulcey white chocolate.

Strawberry milk chocolate kisses

Add 15 g (½ oz) freeze-dried strawberry powder to the marshmallow while whisking, replace the raspberry jam with strawberry, and dip the kisses into milk chocolate.

Blackberry and pink peppercorn kisses

Add ½ teaspoon ground pink peppercorns to the biscuit dough along with the flour, add 25 g (1 oz) freeze-dried blackberry powder to the marshmallow, replace the raspberry jam with blackberry jam and use a 70% (or higher) dark chocolate to coat the kisses.

Iced VoVo™ biscuits

Makes 18

Here's another quintessential Australian icon of a cookie (can you tell that I walked down the supermarket biscuit aisle when looking for inspiration for this book?), but I have a confession to make: I never ate these growing up. I don't know what it was, but the chocolate-covered cookies just sang my name a little louder. In fact, 2023 was a memorable one for me, not because my son was born, or I wrote this book, but because it was the first time I had an Iced VoVo.

200 g (7 oz) plain (all-purpose) flour, plus extra for dusting
15 g (½ oz) milk powder
½ teaspoon baking powder
Pinch of salt
100 g (3½ oz) unsalted butter, softened
80 g (2¾ oz) icing (confectioners') sugar, plus extra for dusting
1 egg yolk
70 g (2½ oz) desiccated coconut, plus extra for decorating
Pink gel food colouring
150 g (5½ oz) white fondant
100 g (3½ oz) good-quality raspberry jam

Combine the flour, milk powder, baking powder and salt in a bowl. Give these dry ingredients a good whisk and set aside.

Using an electric mixer fitted with the paddle attachment, cream the butter, icing sugar and egg yolk until light and fluffy. Add the flour mixture followed by the coconut and mix until just combined.

Wrap the dough in plastic wrap and place in the fridge for 1–2 hours.

Line two baking trays with baking paper or silicone baking mats.

Roll out the chilled dough on a lightly floured bench until 3–4 mm (⅛–³⁄₁₆ inch) thick. Using an 8 x 3 cm (3¼ x 1¼ inch) rectangular crinkle cutter, cut out the cookies and place them on the trays. Chill for 15–20 minutes to help prevent spreading during baking.

Preheat the oven to 160°C (315°F) fan-forced.

Bake the cookies for 12–15 minutes or until the edges are lightly browned. Allow them to cool on the trays for 10 minutes (but leave the oven on) before transferring to a wire rack to cool completely.

Knead the food colouring into the fondant until you achieve your desired colour – a pale pink is perfect here. Dust the bench with icing sugar and roll out the fondant until 2–3 mm (¹⁄₁₆–⅛ inch) thick. Cut the fondant into 7 x 1 cm (2¾ x ½ inch) strips.

Place two fondant strips on each biscuit and return to the oven for 1–2 minutes or until the fondant begins to melt onto the biscuit. (It will just soften; be sure not to overbake as the fondant will seal and the coconut won't stick.)

Remove the biscuits from the oven and immediately sprinkle the extra coconut over the fondant. Place the jam in a piping bag fitted with a small round nozzle and pipe a thin strip of jam down the centre of each cookie. Allow the cookies to cool completely before eating. Pretty as a picture.

Mint Slice™ biscuits, three ways

Makes 16

Since we're deep diving into quintessential Aussie chocolate biscuits, it would be remiss of me to leave out the MVP, the mint slice. Plot twist: I've given you the mint version (the OG), but have also flipped this classic on its head by changing the fondant flavour with passionfruit and strawberry. Why stop there, though? You could use any of your favourites!

The biscuit dough is best made a day in advance, refrigerated overnight and then massaged back into a pliable, workable dough when you are ready to use it.

110 g (3¾ oz) unsalted
  butter, softened
90 g (3¼ oz) icing
  (confectioners') sugar
1 egg
Pinch of salt
160 g (5½ oz) plain
  (all-purpose) flour
40 g (1½ oz) dark cocoa
  powder

Fondant filling
400 g (14 oz) white fondant
Flavouring extract of your
  choice (I've used mint,
  passionfruit and
  strawberry)
Food colouring to match
  your extract (optional)

Chocolate coating
400 g (14 oz) dark
  chocolate
1 teaspoon neutral-
  flavoured oil, such
  as rice bran oil

Using an electric mixer fitted with the paddle attachment, mix the butter, icing sugar, egg and salt until evenly combined and smooth – you don't want aeration here, just a nice cohesive mass. Be sure to scrape down the side of the bowl to ensure there are no streaks of butter and the egg is completely incorporated.

Add the flour and cocoa and mix until the ingredients come together to a soft dough.

Wrap the dough in plastic wrap and place in the fridge for at least 1 hour, but preferably overnight. (This will help reduce spreading during baking.)

Preheat the oven to 180°C (350°F) fan-forced. Line two baking trays with baking paper or silicone baking mats.

Roll out the dough until 3–4 mm (⅛–³⁄₁₆ in) thick. (I like to do this between two sheets of baking paper, which ensures that you don't incorporate more flour into the mixture and also that your cookies don't come out of the oven with a coating of flour all over them.) Using a 5–6 cm (2–2½ inch) cutter, cut the dough into rounds and place them on the baking trays.

Bake the biscuits for 12–14 minutes or until just beginning to brown at the edges. Allow them to cool completely.

Meanwhile, make the fondant filling. If you're making the three different flavours as I've done here, divide the fondant into thirds and knead in 1–2 drops of flavouring extract (or to taste) and the correlating colouring, if using. Roll out the fondant between two pieces of baking paper until 2–3 mm (1/16–1/8 inch) thick, then cut out rounds the same size as the biscuit bases. (If the fondant is too soft to handle, you can put it in the freezer to firm up.) Top each biscuit with a round of fondant.

For the chocolate coating, combine the chocolate and oil in a microwave-safe bowl. Heat on medium in 30-second intervals, stirring in between, until completely melted. This will create a slightly softer chocolate coating.

Dip an entire biscuit into the chocolate coating and scrape the base across the rim of the bowl to remove the excess chocolate. Repeat with the remaining biscuits. (Alternatively, you can line up the biscuits on a wire rack over a baking tray and pour the chocolate over the cookies, ensuring the sides are covered. The first option will give a neater look, but the second option is quicker and easier – the choice is yours!) Gently press the back of a fork into the top of the chocolate to create ridges. Place the biscuits in the fridge to set before diving in (but store any leftovers at room temperature).

Pictured overleaf

Apple pie cookies

Makes 18

Something you may not realise when it comes to cookies is that literally anything can be baked into cookie form. Take these apple pie cookies: we start with a base not too dissimilar from my chocolate-chip cookie recipe and turn it on its head. Finely diced fresh green apples add tartness and freshness, and we pay homage to the original (and flawless) dessert that is apple pie, by baking a cinnamon crumble on top. Warm spices and soft, tart apple pieces encased in a crisp (but soft in the centre) cookie. Perfection.

250 g (9 oz) plain
   (all-purpose) flour
1 teaspoon ground cinnamon
½ teaspoon bicarbonate
   of soda (baking soda)
½ teaspoon baking powder
½ teaspoon sea salt flakes
150 g (5½ oz) unsalted
   butter, softened
130 g (4½ oz) brown sugar
120 g (4¼ oz) caster
   (superfine) sugar
1 egg, at room temperature
1 teaspoon vanilla bean
   paste
2 green apples, peeled and
   cut into 2 mm (1/16 inch) dice

Crumble topping
60 g (2¼ oz) unsalted butter,
   softened
100 g (3½ oz) plain
   (all-purpose) flour
50 g (1¾ oz) caster
   (superfine) sugar

Sugar drizzle
100 g (3½ oz) icing
   (confectioners') sugar
1–2 tablespoons milk or
   cream

Preheat the oven to 170°C (325°F) fan-forced. Line two baking trays with baking paper or silicone baking mats.

Combine the flour, cinnamon, bicarbonate of soda, baking powder and salt in a bowl. Give these ingredients a good whisk and set aside.

Using an electric mixer fitted with the paddle attachment, cream the butter, brown sugar, caster sugar, egg and vanilla for 1–2 minutes or until just combined. Add the dry ingredients and mix until just combined before adding the apple pieces. Give a final mix to incorporate the apple into the dough.

For the crumble topping, combine the butter, flour and caster sugar in a bowl and rub together with your fingertips until a sandy mixture forms.

Roll the dough into balls, using 50 g (1¾ oz) dough for each one, and place them on the baking trays, leaving plenty of room for spreading. Top each ball with 1 tablespoon of the crumble topping mixture.

Bake the cookies for 17–18 minutes or until they are golden brown around the edges but still pale towards the centre. To get your cookies perfectly round, see my tips on page 12.

For the sugar drizzle, put the icing sugar in a bowl and mix in the milk or cream until the mixture has the consistency of thickened (whipping) cream.

Dip a fork into the drizzle and run it quickly back and forth over the cookies. Let the drizzle set for 1–2 hours at room temperature (or just dive in now – there are no rules!).

Twixie Twix™

Makes 12

Growing up, my all-time favourite chocolate bar was a Twix bar. Something about the sandy shortbread with the caramel chocolate combo just did it for me, but I also loved them because they were a staple in my baba's pantry – a little sweety treaty when I stayed at her house – and so they will forever have a place in my heart.

95 g (3¼ oz) unsalted
  butter
90 g (3¼ oz) caster
  (superfine) sugar
2 egg yolks
130 g (4½ oz) plain
  (all-purpose) flour,
  plus extra for dusting
2½ teaspoons baking
  powder
½ teaspoon salt
150 g (5½ oz) milk
  chocolate, tempered
  (see page 17)

Caramel filling
120 ml (3¾ fl oz) thickened
  (whipping) cream
225 g (8 oz) caster
  (superfine) sugar
1 teaspoon salt
125 g (4½ oz) unsalted
  butter
1 teaspoon vanilla bean
  paste

Using an electric mixer fitted with the paddle attachment, cream the butter and sugar until combined – you're not looking for this to be light and fluffy. Add the egg yolks and mix until combined, then mix in the flour, baking powder and salt.

Wrap the dough in plastic wrap and place in the fridge to firm up and chill for 1–2 hours.

Preheat the oven to 180°C (350°F) fan-forced. Brush or spray a silicone or metal muffin tin with oil.

Roll out the chilled dough on a lightly floured bench until 1 cm (½ inch) thick, stopping and rotating as you go to ensure it isn't sticking to the bench (and adding small amounts of flour if it is). Using a 5–6 cm (2–2½ inch) cutter, cut out 12 rounds and use them to line the muffin holes.

Bake the cookie bases for 12 minutes, then remove them from the oven. Take a spoon, a small glass or a ¼ cup measuring cup and press it into the cookie base to form an indent with a 5 mm (¼ inch) border. Return the cookie bases to the oven for a further 5–7 minutes or until cooked through. If the indents puff up again, simply press them down a second time. Leave the cookie bases to cool in the tin for 10 minutes before transferring to a wire rack to cool completely.

For the filling, pour the cream into a small saucepan and bring to a simmer.

continued...

Meanwhile, in a large saucepan, stir the sugar over medium heat until it has melted and begins to caramelise. (This is a dry caramel – i.e. there is no water – so you don't have to worry about it crystallising.) Continue stirring the caramel until it reaches a deep amber colour, then remove from the heat and carefully pour in the warm cream (it will splatter, which is why it's best to use a large saucepan). Once the cream is incorporated, add the salt, butter and vanilla. Return the caramel to the heat and cook until it reaches 118°C (244°F) on a sugar thermometer.

Carefully pour the hot caramel into the indents in the cookie bases. Allow the caramel to cool completely.

Spread 1–2 teaspoons of the tempered chocolate over the caramel. Leave the cookies to set completely at room temperature.

Matcha, white chocolate and raspberry cookies

Makes 18

I'm not going to lie to you, matcha isn't my favourite flavour. I find it a touch too earthy for my tastes; however, there's an exception to every rule. The sweetness of white chocolate and the tartness of raspberries complement the earthy tones of matcha here perfectly, making for a well-rounded, balanced cookie that is totally moreish.

250 g (9 oz) plain (all-purpose) flour
2 teaspoons matcha powder, plus extra for dusting
½ teaspoon bicarbonate of soda (baking soda)
½ teaspoon baking powder
½ teaspoon salt
160 g (5½ oz) unsalted butter, softened
130 g (4½ oz) brown sugar
100 g (3½ oz) caster (superfine) sugar
1 egg, at room temperature
2 teaspoons vanilla bean paste
250 g (9 oz) white chocolate chips
125 g (4½ oz) fresh or frozen raspberries
10 g (¼ oz) freeze-dried raspberries, to garnish

Preheat the oven to 180°C (350°F) fan-forced. Line two baking trays with baking paper or silicone baking mats.

Sift the flour, matcha, bicarbonate of soda, baking powder and salt into a bowl.

Using an electric mixer fitted with the paddle attachment, cream the butter, brown sugar, caster sugar, egg and vanilla until just combined. Add the flour mixture along with 200 g (7 oz) of the white chocolate chips and the raspberries and mix until just combined. Do not overmix as the raspberries will break down in the dough.

Roll the dough into balls, using 50 g (1¾ oz) dough for each one, and place them on the baking trays. These gals will spread, so give them space to do their thing.

Bake the cookies for 14–15 minutes or until they are caramelised around the edges while still soft towards the centre. To get your cookies perfectly round, see my tips on page 12.

While the cookies are still warm, sift a fine layer of matcha powder over the top, then sprinkle with the remaining white chocolate chips and the freeze-dried raspberries. Allow them to cool completely on the trays.

Pecan pie shortbread bars

Makes 14

Pecan pie is a true thing of beauty: warming, rich, treacly flavours with the delightful crunch of pecans throughout. I don't bake with pecans all that often so when I do, in a bar like this, it's a real delight.

170 g (5¾ oz) unsalted butter, softened
90 g (3¼ oz) caster (superfine) sugar
1 teaspoon vanilla bean paste
265 g (9¼ oz) plain (all-purpose) flour
½ teaspoon baking powder
Pinch of salt

Caramel pecan filling
300 g (10½ oz) golden syrup
150 g (5½ oz) caster (superfine) sugar
4 eggs
60 g (2¼ oz) unsalted butter, melted
2 teaspoons vanilla bean paste
1 teaspoon salt
180 g (6 oz) pecans, roasted and roughly chopped

Preheat the oven to 160°C (315°F) fan-forced. Line a 25 cm (10 inch) square cake tin with baking paper.

Using an electric mixer fitted with the paddle attachment, mix the butter, sugar and vanilla until just combined. Add the flour, baking powder and salt and mix until the shortbread dough just comes together.

Press the dough into the cake tin in an even layer. Bake for 12–14 minutes or until lightly golden brown at the edges. Allow the base to cool slightly while you prepare the filling.

For the filling, combine the golden syrup, sugar, eggs, melted butter, vanilla and salt in a bowl and whisk until smooth. Add the pecans and stir to combine.

Pour the filling over the shortbread and bake for 1 hour. Allow to cool completely in the tin before slicing into 3 x 9 cm (1¼ x 3½ inch) bars.

Baklava cookies

Makes 32

A little riff on a classic Greek dessert (and my mum's personal favourite). These cookies are one part melomakarona (a classic Greek cookie) and one part baklava; they're doused in a thick honey syrup and just get better and better as they sit and absorb that sugary goodness.

400 g (14 oz) plain (all-purpose) flour
100 g (3½ oz) fine semolina
1 teaspoon bicarbonate of soda (baking soda)
1 teaspoon baking powder
250 g (9 oz) unsalted butter, softened
50 ml (1¾ fl oz) neutral-flavoured oil, such as rice bran oil
100 g (3½ oz) caster (superfine) sugar
1 egg
120 ml (3¾ fl oz) orange juice
100 g (3½ oz) chopped walnuts
100 g (3½ oz) chopped pistachios

Preheat the oven to 180°C (350°F) fan-forced. Line two baking trays with baking paper or silicone baking mats.

Start by baking the pastry for the topping. Lay one piece of filo on a baking tray and brush liberally with melted butter before topping with the second sheet of filo. Brush the top of the filo with the remaining butter and bake for 10–15 minutes or until the pastry is completely golden brown. Set aside to cool.

Meanwhile, combine the flour, semolina, bicarbonate of soda and baking powder in a bowl. Give these ingredients a good whisk and set aside.

Using an electric mixer fitted with the paddle attachment, cream the butter, oil and sugar until light and fluffy. Add the egg and mix to combine. Gradually add the flour mixture along with the orange juice. Mix until the dough pulls away from the side of the bowl cleanly. Finally, add the nuts and mix until just combined, being careful not to completely crush them.

Roll the dough into balls, using 30 g (1 oz) dough for each one, then flatten the balls slightly and place them on the baking trays, allowing room for spreading. Prick each round with a fork three times (this allows the syrup to soak in more easily after baking).

Bake the cookies for 20–25 minutes or until golden brown.

Baklava topping

2 sheets filo pastry
60 g (2¼ oz) unsalted
  butter, melted
50 g (1¾ oz) walnuts,
  crushed
50 g (1¾ oz) pistachios,
  crushed

Spiced syrup

300 g (10½ oz) caster
  (superfine) sugar
150 g (5½ oz) honey
4 cinnamon sticks
20 cloves
Rind of 2 oranges, peeled
  into strips
Juice of 2 oranges

Meanwhile, for the spiced syrup, combine all of the ingredients in a saucepan with 200 ml (7 fl oz) water. Bring to the boil to dissolve the sugar, then boil for another 2–3 minutes or until slightly reduced. Turn off the heat and set the syrup aside for 10–15 minutes to allow the spices to steep.

Allow the cookies to cool slightly before completely submerging them in the syrup for 10–15 seconds, then remove and drain on a wire rack.

Crush the cooled filo and combine it with the crushed nuts in a bowl. Top each cookie with ½–1 teaspoon of the filo and nut mixture.

Pictured overleaf

Strawberry and cream bar cookies

Makes 12

These cookies encompass everything I love in a springtime dessert: they're fresh, tart, flavoursome and exciting. They may just be a top-ten favourite recipe of mine. The magic lies in the freeze-dried strawberries, which can be somewhat difficult to find. Online is my jam, or check out the nut or baby food section of your local supermarket – they're often sold as a toddler snack. If you can't get hold of them, you can try replacing them with chopped fresh or frozen strawberries.

220 g (7¾ oz) plain
(all-purpose) flour
½ teaspoon bicarbonate
of soda (baking soda)
½ teaspoon baking
powder
¼ teaspoon sea salt flakes
160 g (5½ oz) unsalted
butter, softened
125 g (4½ oz) brown sugar
100 g (3½ oz) caster
(superfine) sugar
1 egg, at room temperature
2 teaspoons vanilla bean
paste
275 g (9¾ oz) white
chocolate chips
40 g (1½ oz) freeze-dried
strawberries

Preheat the oven to 160°C (315°F) fan-forced. Line a 20 cm (8 inch) square cake tin with baking paper.

Combine the flour, bicarbonate of soda, baking powder and salt in a bowl. Give these ingredients a good whisk and set aside.

Using an electric mixer fitted with the paddle attachment, cream the butter, brown sugar, caster sugar, egg and vanilla until just combined. Add the flour mixture and 200 g (7 oz) of the white chocolate chips and mix until just combined. Finally, add half of the freeze-dried strawberries and gently mix to incorporate.

Press the dough evenly into the tin and bake for 24–26 minutes or until caramelised around the edges while still soft and blond towards the centre. While the cookie slab is still warm from the oven, scatter the remaining white chocolate chips over the top, then top with the remaining freeze-dried strawberries (I like to crush some of the strawberries so you get some powdery texture along with the pieces). The residual warmth will slightly melt and secure the topping. Allow the slab to cool completely in the tin before slicing it into 3 x 9 cm (1¼ x 3½ inch) bars.

Blueberry muffin top cookies

Makes 14

This recipe draws inspiration from one of the best *Seinfeld* episodes of all time: 'The Muffin Tops'. (If you don't know it, get to know it. It's a 10 out of 10.) These are a soft cookie; think everything you love about the top of a muffin – the slightly crisp cakeness – rebranded as a cookie. Top of the muffin to you!

210 g (7½ oz) plain
   (all-purpose) flour
½ teaspoon bicarbonate
   of soda (baking soda)
½ teaspoon baking
   powder
¼ teaspoon sea salt flakes
160 g (5½ oz) unsalted
   butter, softened
125 g (4½ oz) brown sugar
100 g (3½ oz) caster
   (superfine) sugar
1 egg, at room temperature
2 teaspoons vanilla bean
   paste
Grated zest of 1 lemon
170 g (5¾ oz) fresh
   blueberries

Crumble topping
110 g (3¾ oz) plain
   (all-purpose) flour
50 g (1¾ oz) caster
   (superfine) sugar
45 g (1½ oz) brown sugar
70 g (2½ oz) unsalted
   butter, softened
Pinch of salt

Preheat the oven to 180°C (350°F) fan-forced. Line two baking trays with baking paper or silicone baking mats.

Combine the flour, bicarbonate of soda, baking powder and salt in a bowl. Give these ingredients a good whisk and set aside.

Using an electric mixer fitted with the paddle attachment, cream the butter, brown sugar, caster sugar, egg, vanilla and lemon zest for 1–2 minutes or until just combined. Add the dry ingredients and mix until just combined, then gently mix in the blueberries.

For the crumble topping, combine all of the ingredients in a bowl and use your fingertips to rub the butter into the dry ingredients.

Roll the dough into balls, using 50 g (1¾ oz) dough for each one, and place on the baking trays. These will spread, so give them space to do their thing.

Bake the cookies for 5 minutes, then remove from the oven and sprinkle 1 tablespoon of the crumble topping on top of each cookie. Return the cookies to the oven to bake for 10 minutes or until caramelised around the edges while still soft and blond towards the centre. Allow them to cool completely on the trays.

Cookimisu

Makes 12

The base of this cookie is not too different to a snickerdoodle, which, to be honest, is not an amazing cookie. The best way I can describe a snickerdoodle is that it's a chocolate chip-less cookie, rolled in sugar (for crunch). I've pimped these up, with coffee in the base and a creamy mascarpone topping to rival the best tiramisu.

1 tablespoon instant coffee
  powder
1 tablespoon warm water
120 g (4¼ oz) unsalted
  butter, softened
200 g (7 oz) brown sugar
2 eggs
1 teaspoon vanilla extract
210 g (7½ oz) plain
  (all-purpose) flour
½ teaspoon bicarbonate
  of soda (baking soda)
½ teaspoon cream of
  tartar
¼ teaspoon salt

Coffee sugar
100 g (3½ oz) caster
  (superfine) sugar
1 heaped tablespoon
  instant coffee powder

Mascarpone swirl
300 g (10½ oz) mascarpone
140 g (5 oz) icing
  (confectioners') sugar
2 teaspoons vanilla bean
  paste
Dark cocoa powder,
  for dusting

Preheat the oven to 180°C (350°F) fan-forced. Line two baking trays with baking paper or silicone baking mats.

Mix the coffee powder with the warm water and stir until the coffee has dissolved.

Using an electric mixer fitted with the paddle attachment, mix the butter, brown sugar and eggs on medium speed until lightened in colour – you don't want aeration here, just a nice cohesive mass. Add the coffee and vanilla and mix until well combined, then mix in the flour, bicarbonate of soda, cream of tartar and salt.

Make the coffee sugar by mixing the caster sugar with the coffee powder in a small bowl.

Roll the dough into balls, using 30 g (1 oz) dough for each one, then roll each ball in the coffee sugar. Place the balls on the baking trays, leaving plenty of room for spreading.

Bake the cookies for 10–12 minutes or until golden brown and delicious. Allow them to cool completely on the trays.

For the mascarpone swirl, mix the mascarpone, icing sugar and vanilla in a small bowl until smooth. Transfer the mascarpone to a piping bag fitted with a 5 mm (¼ inch) round nozzle.

To assemble, pipe the marscapone on top of the cookies in a spiral and smooth it into a swirl with the back of a spoon before dusting with cocoa powder. These cookies are best enjoyed the same day they're made.

Rhubarb lattice pie cookies

Makes 14

Butter sable cookies filled with luscious rhubarb jam and topped with more of that sable dough – pretty as a picture and delicious to boot! These beauties may look intimidating, but really they're just sandwich cookies with a lattice top. Latticing is not overly difficult once you get the hang of it. The trick? Keep the dough chilled for easier handling – if it's getting difficult to work with, pop it back in the fridge for 15 minutes.

160 g (5½ oz) unsalted butter, softened
140 g (5 oz) caster (superfine) sugar
1 egg
1 teaspoon vanilla bean paste
½ teaspoon salt
1 teaspoon ground cinnamon
300 g (10½ oz) plain (all-purpose) flour, plus extra for dusting
160 g (5½ oz) good-quality rhubarb jam (or any jam you love)

Using an electric mixer fitted with the paddle attachment, mix the butter and sugar on low speed until smooth – you don't want this to be light and fluffy, just a nice cohesive mass. Add the egg, vanilla, salt and cinnamon and mix to combine. Scrape down the side of the bowl to ensure there are no large streaks of butter that will affect the final cookies. Add the flour, in two batches, and mix until completely incorporated.

Divide the dough in half, wrap each portion in plastic wrap and place in the fridge for at least 2 hours. (This will help reduce spreading during baking. You can make the dough the day prior and refrigerate it overnight, if preferred.)

Preheat the oven to 180°C (350°F) fan-forced. Line two baking trays with baking paper or silicone baking mats.

Roll out one portion of the chilled dough on a lightly floured bench until 2–3 mm (1⁄16–1⁄8 inch) thick, stopping and rotating as you go to ensure it isn't sticking to the bench (and adding small amounts of flour if it is). Using a 5 cm (2 inch) round cutter (fluted is cute, too!), cut out 14 rounds and place them on the baking trays.

Bake these base cookies for 6–8 minutes or until lightly golden brown. Allow them to cool completely on the trays.

Roll out the second dough portion and cut it into 7–8 mm (3⁄8 inch) wide strips, around 2 mm (1⁄16 inch) thick. Weave the strips of dough to achieve a lattice pattern (there are some great guides on the internet). Once you have a large sheet of latticed dough, use your cutter to cut out another 14 dough rounds.

Bake the lattice cookies for 8–10 minutes or until lightly golden brown. Allow them to cool completely on the trays.

To assemble, place a teaspoon of the rhubarb jam in the centre of the base cookies and top with the lattice cookies.

Hazelnut praline squiggles

Makes 28

When I thought about writing a second book, dedicated entirely to cookies, I had just had my second baby, Mac. I was at my family's beach house, one week postpartum, and decided it was the perfect time to begin playing around with recipes. This was the first thing I baked. Of course, in my newborn, post-C-section haze, I didn't write down the recipe, and this version is as close to the original as I can remember. The praline can be made 1–2 weeks ahead and stored in a sealed container in the fridge.

240 g (8½ oz) hazelnuts, roasted and peeled
150 g (5½ oz) plain (all-purpose) flour
140 g (5 oz) caster (superfine) sugar
45 g (1½ oz) cornflour (cornstarch)
½ teaspoon salt
140 g (5 oz) unsalted butter, softened
1 egg yolk
1 teaspoon vanilla extract
100 g (3½ oz) hazelnuts, roasted, peeled and chopped
400 g (14 oz) dark or milk chocolate
100 g (3½ oz) white chocolate

Hazelnut praline paste
150 g (5½ oz) hazelnuts, roasted and peeled
150 g (5½ oz) caster (superfine) sugar

Line two baking trays with baking paper or silicone baking mats.

In a food processor, blitz the nuts until fine – don't overdo it because you'll end up with hazelnut butter. Add the flour, sugar, cornflour and salt and pulse until just combined, then add the butter, egg yolk and vanilla and blitz until the mixture comes together as a ball. (If your butter isn't soft enough, the mixture will appear sandy; keep blitzing until it comes together.)

Roll out the dough on a lightly floured bench until 3–4 mm (⅛–³⁄₁₆ inch) thick. If the dough is feeling a little soft/challenging to work with, you can pop it in the fridge for 30 minutes to firm up. Using a 5 cm (2 inch) cutter, cut the dough into rounds and place them on the baking trays. Pop the cookies in the fridge for 30 minutes to help reduce spreading during baking.

Meanwhile, preheat the oven to 180°C (350°F) fan-forced.

Bake the cookies for 8–10 minutes or until lightly golden brown. Allow to cool.

For the hazelnut praline paste, spread the hazelnuts on a baking tray lined with baking paper. Put the sugar in a saucepan over medium heat. The sugar will begin to caramelise at the edges. At this stage you can begin stirring until the sugar is completely caramelised – a deep amber colour is the goal. Pour the hot sugar over the hazelnuts and leave to set completely, about 30 minutes.

Break up the praline, transfer it to a food processor and blitz until the praline liquifies; the time for this will depend on the strength of your processor.

Transfer the praline paste to a piping bag and trim off the tip. Pipe about 1 teaspoon of the paste on top of each biscuit and sprinkle with the chopped hazelnuts. Place the biscuits in the freeze to set for 15 minutes.

Temper the chocolate in separate bowls, following the guide on page 17.

Dip each biscuit into the tempered dark or milk chocolate, scraping the base of the biscuit across the rim of the bowl to remove the excess chocolate. Transfer the tempered white chocolate to a piping bag and trim off the tip. Create squiggles by zigzagging back and forth over the top of each biscuit.

Allow to set completely, either at room temperature or in the fridge, before serving.

Pictured overleaf

Raspberry and white chocolate cornflake cookies

Makes 12

I developed this recipe after a trip to the supermarket. I was browsing the chocolate aisle (obviously) and stumbled across a white chocolate block containing cornflakes and coconut. I bought it, raced home and baked a bunch of cookies before deciding they needed a fresh little pop to truly make them sing. Enter the raspberry. These guys almost* qualify as breakfast.

220 g (7¾ oz) plain (all-purpose) flour
½ teaspoon bicarbonate of soda (baking soda)
½ teaspoon baking powder
¼ teaspoon sea salt flakes
150 g (5½ oz) unsalted butter, softened
125 g (4½ oz) brown sugar
100 g (3½ oz) caster (superfine) sugar
1 egg, at room temperature
2 teaspoons vanilla bean paste
40 g (1½ oz) shredded coconut
25 g (1 oz) cornflakes
125 g (4½ oz) fresh raspberries
255 g (9 oz) white chocolate chips
15 g (½ oz) freeze-dried raspberries (optional)

Preheat the oven to 180°C (350°F) fan-forced. Line two baking trays with baking paper or silicone baking mats.

Combine the flour, bicarbonate of soda, baking powder and salt in a bowl. Give these ingredients a good whisk and set aside.

Using an electric mixer fitted with the paddle attachment, cream the butter, brown and caster sugars, egg and vanilla until smooth and lightly aerated. Add the flour mixture and mix until just combined, then add the coconut, cornflakes, raspberries and 180 g (6 oz) of the white chocolate chips. Give the dough a final, gentle mix on low speed, being careful not to completely crush the cornflakes and raspberries.

Roll the dough into balls, using 75 g (2½ oz) dough for each one, and place on the baking trays. These will spread, so give them plenty of room.

Bake the cookies for 20–22 minutes or until caramelised around the edges while still soft and blond towards the centre. The juiciness of the raspberries means these take a little longer to bake than your ordinary chocolate-chip cookie. While the cookies are still warm, scatter them with the remaining white chocolate chips before crumbling the freeze-dried raspberries over the top. Allow the cookies to cool completely on the trays.

*They definitely don't.

Blackberry cheesecake cookies

Makes 16

Once you learn a solid cookie base recipe – i.e. the chocolate-chip cookie without chocolate chips – you will become an unstoppable cookie master! These are a variation of blackberry and white chocolate-chip cookies, stuffed with a little lemony cheesecake action.

350 g (12 oz) plain (all-purpose) flour
1 teaspoon bicarbonate of soda (baking soda)
½ teaspoon salt
210 g (7½ oz) unsalted butter, softened
80 g (2¾ oz) brown sugar
120 g (4¼ oz) caster (superfine) sugar
1 egg, at room temperature
1 teaspoon vanilla bean paste
200 g (7 oz) white chocolate chips
125 g (4½ oz) fresh blackberries, roughly chopped

Cheesecake inserts
300 g (10½ oz) cream cheese, softened
60 g (2¼ oz) icing (confectioners') sugar
2 teaspoons vanilla bean paste
Grated zest of 2 lemons

Preheat the oven to 200°C (400°F) fan-forced. Line two baking trays with baking paper or silicone baking mats.

For the cheesecake inserts, combine all of the ingredients in a bowl and whisk until smooth. Spoon the mixture into blobs on another baking tray, using 2 teaspoons for each, and freeze while you prepare the cookie dough.

Combine the flour, bicarbonate of soda and salt in a bowl and give these ingredients a good whisk, then set aside.

Using an electric mixer fitted with the paddle attachment, cream the butter, brown and caster sugars, egg and vanilla until smooth and lightly aerated. Add the flour mixture along with the chocolate chips and mix until just combined. Gently mix in the chopped blackberries on low speed – don't overmix here as the blackberries will leach their colour into the dough and turn it grey.

Roll the dough into balls, using 70 g (2½ oz) dough for each. Flatten each ball in the palm of your hand, place one of the frozen cheesecake inserts in the centre and completely encase the cheesecake within the ball of cookie dough. Place the balls on the baking trays, leaving plenty of room for spreading.

Bake the cookies for 15–16 minutes or until caramelised around the edges while still soft and blond towards the centre. To get your cookies perfectly round, see my tips on page 12.

Raspberry rhubarb crumble bars

Makes 9

Many of us were lucky enough to grow up with our mamas baking a crumble bar of some type. Traditionally, the bars are spread with jam before the crumble topping is added, but the addition of fresh fruit really brings these to life. You could make these with any fruit and jam combination you love: fig jam with raspberries, apricot jam with apricots, plum jam studded with blackberries – the world is your oyster.

170 g (5¾ oz) unsalted
  butter, softened
90 g (3¼ oz) caster
  (superfine) sugar
1 teaspoon vanilla bean
  paste
265 g (9¼ oz) plain
  (all-purpose) flour
½ teaspoon baking
  powder
Pinch of salt

**Raspberry rhubarb
filling**
4 large rhubarb stalks,
  diced
100 g (3½ oz) good-quality
  raspberry jam
125 g (4½ oz) fresh
  raspberries

Crumble topping
110 g (3¾ oz) plain
  (all-purpose) flour
50 g (1¾ oz) caster
  (superfine) sugar
45 g (1½ oz) brown sugar
70 g (2½ oz) unsalted
  butter, softened
Pinch of salt

Preheat the oven to 180°C (350°F) fan-forced. Line a 20 cm (8 inch) square cake tin with baking paper.

Using an electric mixer fitted with the paddle attachment, mix the butter, sugar and vanilla until just combined. Add the flour, baking powder and salt and mix until the shortbread dough just comes together.

Press the dough evenly into the cake tin and bake for 20 minutes or until lightly golden brown at the edges. Allow the base to cool slightly while you prepare the filling.

For the raspberry rhubarb filling, mix the rhubarb, raspberry jam and raspberries together in a large bowl. Top the shortbread with the filling and set aside.

For the crumble topping, combine all of the ingredients in a bowl and use your fingertips to rub them together until the butter is mixed into the dry ingredients. Generously sprinkle the crumble topping over the raspberry rhubarb filling.

Return the slice to the oven for 30–35 minutes or until the fruit has cooked down and become jammy and the crumble is a beautiful golden brown. Allow to cool in the tin before slicing into 6.5 cm (2½ inch) squares.

Pandan and coconut cookies

Makes 14

Pandan is one of those beautiful ingredients that gives an incredible, vibrant colour along with a unique flavour that can't be replaced. Many people describe it as a vanilla-type flavour, but to me, it is more reminiscent of a heavy vanilla custard – rich, fragrant and just so good. If you haven't used pandan before, or don't know where to get it, an Asian grocer is your best bet (otherwise google is your best friend here!). My favourite brand is Koepoe Koepoe and is what I used to test these beauties. If you're using a different brand of pandan, you may need to adjust the recipe to taste.

100 g (3½ oz) desiccated coconut
200 g (7 oz) plain (all-purpose) flour
½ teaspoon bicarbonate of soda (baking soda)
½ teaspoon baking powder
½ teaspoon sea salt flakes
160 g (5½ oz) unsalted butter, softened
130 g (4½ oz) brown sugar
100 g (3½ oz) caster (superfine) sugar
1 egg, at room temperature
1 teaspoon pandan liquid essence
200 g (7 oz) white chocolate, melted

Preheat the oven to 180°C (350°F) fan-forced. Line two baking trays with baking paper or silicone baking mats.

Spread the coconut over one of the trays and toast in the oven for 4–5 minutes or until lightly golden brown. Set aside to cool completely.

Combine the flour, bicarbonate of soda, baking powder and salt in a bowl. Give these ingredients a good whisk and set aside.

Using an electric mixer fitted with the paddle attachment, cream the butter, brown sugar, caster sugar, egg and pandan essence until lightly aerated. Add 70 g (2½ oz) of the toasted coconut along with the flour mixture and mix until just combined.

Roll the dough into balls, using 50 g (1¾ oz) dough for each one, and place on the baking trays, allowing plenty of room for spreading.

Bake the cookies for 12–13 minutes or until they are caramelised around the edges while still soft and blond (and by blond, I mean pale green!) towards the centre. Halfway through the baking time, shape the cookies into perfect rounds (see page 12) and return them to the oven. Allow the cookies to cool on the trays for about 10 minutes before transferring to a wire rack to cool completely.

Fill a piping bag with the melted white chocolate and trim off a tiny corner. Moving the bag quickly back and forth, decorate the cookies. While the chocolate is still runny, sprinkle the rest of the toasted coconut over the cookies. Allow the chocolate to set before eating.

Sticky date whoopie pies

Makes 14

Sticky date is god-tier dessert – so simple in its preparation yet so wildly satisfying in its delivery. I just had to think of a way to work those beautiful flavours that we all love into cookie format. Enter the whoopie pie, or cake cookie.

120 g (4¼ oz) dates, finely chopped
100 ml (3½ fl oz) boiling water
1½ teaspoons bicarbonate of soda (baking soda)
125 g (4½ oz) unsalted butter, softened
170 g (5¾ oz) brown sugar
1 egg
250 g (9 oz) plain (all-purpose) flour
50 ml (1¾ fl oz) milk

Golden syrup buttercream
100 g (3½ oz) unsalted butter, softened
75 g (2½ oz) icing (confectioners') sugar
150 g (5½ oz) golden syrup
1 teaspoon vanilla bean paste
½ teaspoon salt

Preheat the oven to 180°C (350°F) fan-forced. Line two baking trays with baking paper or silicone baking mats.

Combine the dates, boiling water and bicarbonate of soda in a bowl and set aside for 5 minutes to allow the dates to soften. If they don't soften enough, you can pop them in the microwave for 30–60 seconds. Using a stick blender, blitz the date mixture until smooth (or mash with the back of a fork) and allow to cool.

Using an electric mixer fitted with the paddle attachment, mix the butter and brown sugar until light and fluffy, around 3–4 minutes. Add the egg and the cooled date purée and mix to combine, then add the flour and milk and mix until the batter is smooth.

Using a medium-sized cookie scoop, scoop uniform balls of the batter onto the baking trays, leaving room for the cookies to spread and rise. Flatten the cookies slightly before baking.

Bake the cookies for 8 minutes or until brown around the edges. Halfway through the baking time, use a round cutter to shape the cookies into perfect rounds (see page 12) and then return them to the oven. Allow the cookies to cool completely on the trays.

For the buttercream, combine the butter, icing sugar and golden syrup in the bowl of the electric mixer. Beat on medium speed until light and fluffy, then mix in the vanilla and salt.

Transfer the buttercream to a piping bag fitted with a 1 cm (½ inch) round nozzle. Pipe a generous tablespoon of the buttercream onto the centre of half the cookies before sandwiching with the remaining cookies.

Lemon, lime and bitters bars

Makes 14

Lemon bars are a classic; LLB is also a classic. Why not get them together and make a dream bake? I love how magical these are – when I'm preparing them I can convince myself that they're never going to work, but then when I slice them and see that perfectly set curd? Magic.

300 g (10½ oz) plain
(all-purpose) flour
80 g (2¾ oz) icing
(confectioners') sugar
1 teaspoon salt
180 g (6 oz) unsalted
butter, softened

Curd topping
300 g (10½ oz) caster
(superfine) sugar
Grated zest of 2 lemons
Grated zest of 1 lime
45 g (1½ oz) plain
(all-purpose) flour
5 eggs
100 ml (3½ fl oz) lemon
juice
90 ml (3 fl oz) lime juice
30 ml (1 fl oz) bitters

Preheat the oven to 180°C (350°F) fan-forced. Line a 20 cm (8 inch) square cake tin with baking paper so that the baking paper is overhanging the sides (to make it easy to remove the finished bars from the tin).

Combine the flour, icing sugar and salt in the bowl of a food processor or electric mixer and briefly pulse to combine. Add the butter and mix until the dough just comes together. (You can also do this step by hand by simply rubbing the butter into the dry ingredients using your fingertips.)

Transfer the dough to the cake tin and use the bottom of a flat glass to press it evenly into the tin.

Bake the base for 20–25 minutes or until golden brown.

For the curd topping, combine the sugar and zests in a large bowl and, using your fingertips, rub the zest into the sugar – this will help release the oils in the zest and amplify the citrus flavour. Add the flour and whisk together. Add the eggs, citrus juices and bitters and whisk until completely combined.

Reduce the oven temperature to 160°C (315°F). Pour the curd over the base and bake for 20–25 minutes or until the curd has just set. Allow the slab to cool completely in the tin, then transfer to the fridge to cool for at least 2 hours (preferably overnight).

Cut the slab into 3 x 9 cm (1¼ x 3½ inch) bars. Store in the fridge.

The
Classy
Gal

Maple shortbread leaves —— 136

Black Forest brookies —— 138

Pistachio and dark chocolate-chip cookies —— 141

Earl Grey millionaire shortbread —— 143

Miso dark chocolate flourless cookies —— 146

Orange creams —— 149

Passionfruit curd macadamia thumbprints —— 150

Passionfruit and chocolate sandwiches —— 152

Bounty™ macarons —— 154

Mango and green tea macarons —— 158

Raspberry parfait macaron sandwiches —— 162

Cinnamon, coffee and macadamia biscotti —— 166

Apricot pistachio crumble bars —— 169

Limoncello spritz bars —— 170

Kingston™ biscuits —— 172

Seed and nut cookies —— 175

Chai-spiced sugar cookies —— 176

Monte Carlo™ biscuits —— 179

Almond and coconut chocolate clusters —— 180

Persian love cookies —— 182

Exactly what, you may ask, is a classy gal cookie? Well, my friends, let me tell you. This gal loves rich flavour profiles and hints of fruits and florals, enjoys a cocktail here and there, and is quite partial to a cup of tea. These cookies are elegant, refined, interesting and unique.

We play around with a few more flavours, and there might be a trip or two in store for you to a specialist deli, nut shop or providore. Think maple sugar, jasmine tea, limoncello, sour cherries and pistachio praline paste. Don't let that deter you, though – these bikkies are a joy to bake and indulge in.

Maple shortbread leaves

Makes 16

I will admit, there are a couple of difficulties with this one: namely, the ingredients. Maple sugar isn't always the easiest item to source. Online is your best friend here, but if you can only find the maple extract, replace the maple sugar with caster (superfine) sugar and boost the maple extract to 2 teaspoons. I've made these delicate little sandwich cookies using a maple-leaf cookie cutter, but you can just use whatever cutters you have on hand.

110 g (3¾ oz) maple sugar
225 g (8 oz) unsalted
   butter, softened
1 teaspoon maple extract
¼ teaspoon salt
380 g (13½ oz) plain
   (all-purpose) flour,
   plus extra for dusting

Maple buttercream
50 g (1¾ oz) unsalted
   butter, softened
50 ml (1¾ fl oz) maple
   syrup
½ teaspoon maple extract
150 g (5½ oz) icing
   (confectioners') sugar
Pinch of salt

Using an electric mixer fitted with the paddle attachment, mix the maple sugar, butter, maple extract and salt until well combined. Add the flour and mix until a dough forms.

Wrap the dough in plastic wrap and pop it in the fridge for 30–60 minutes to firm up. This will make it much easier to roll and emboss the flower pattern onto the dough.

Preheat the oven to 150°C (300°F) fan-forced. Line two baking trays with baking paper or silicone baking mats.

Roll out the dough on a lightly floured bench until 3–4 mm (⅛–³⁄₁₆ inch) thick. Use a maple leaf embosser tool and stamp to cut the dough into leaves. (Or cut the dough into any shape you like.) Place the leaves on the baking trays.

Bake the cookies for 17–18 minutes. You don't necessarily want them to colour while baking, so they will still be quite blond. Allow the cookies to cool on the trays for 10 minutes before transferring to a wire rack to cool completely.

For the buttercream, combine all of the ingredients in the bowl of an electric mixer fitted with the whisk attachment and beat until smooth.

Transfer the buttercream to a piping bag fitted with a 1 cm (½ inch) round nozzle. Pipe 1 teaspoon of the buttercream onto the centre of half the cookies and sandwich with the remaining cookies.

Black Forest brookies

Makes 6
Gluten free

My best friend Tammy always asks for Black Forest cake for her birthday. One year, I brought the goods: I went totally over the top with layers of chocolate mousse, sponge, a cherry jelly and vanilla crémeux – it was big and bold and totally non-traditional. These brookie sandwiches are just that: big, bold and totally non-traditional. Note, if you can't find buckwheat flour for the brownie cookies, you can replace it with cornflour (cornstarch) in the same quantity.

Start this recipe a day ahead, if possible, to allow the chocolate chantilly time to set and chill thoroughly.

1 batch Buckwheat chocolate brownie cookies (page 48)

Chocolate chantilly
150 g (5½ oz) dark chocolate, chopped
500 ml (17 fl oz) thickened (whipping) cream
200 ml (7 fl oz) thick (double) cream
2 teaspoons vanilla bean paste

Cherry compote
300 g (10½ oz) jar morello cherries, in their juice
75 g (2½ oz) caster (superfine) sugar
1 teaspoon cornflour (cornstarch)
1 teaspoon vanilla extract
2 tablespoons kirsch liqueur

For the chantilly, combine the chocolate and 200 ml (7 fl oz) of the thickened cream in a microwave-safe bowl and heat on high in 30-second intervals, stirring in between, until completely melted. Add the rest of the thickened cream, the thick cream and the vanilla and whisk until smooth. Set this in the fridge until completely chilled (preferably overnight).

For the cherry compote, tip the cherries and liquid from the jar into a saucepan and add the sugar, cornflour, vanilla and kirsch. Cook over medium heat until the cherries have softened slightly and the juices have thickened (thank you, cornflour!). Allow this mixture to cool completely.

Transfer the chilled chocolate and cream mixture to the bowl of an electric mixer fitted with the whisk attachment and whisk on medium speed until thickened to firm peaks.

Transfer the chocolate chantilly to a piping bag fitted with a Wilton #1M star nozzle or a 1 cm (½ inch) star nozzle.

Pipe a decent amount of chantilly around the edge of one of the brownie cookies and fill the cavity with the cherry compote. Top with a second cookie and gently press to seal. Repeat with the remaining cookies. These are best eaten the day they are filled, but can be stored in the fridge for up to 2 days.

Pistachio and dark chocolate-chip cookies

Makes 20

Another day, another chocolate-chip cookie, but this one is as classy as they come. While it may be rustic looking, the flavours of good-quality dark chocolate and pistachio are elegant and complex. To get your cookies as green as these, you'll need to find Iranian pistachios; they're picked while not quite ripe so they haven't had the chance to lose their bright green colour.

80 g (2¾ oz) pistachios
200 g (7 oz) plain
  (all-purpose) flour
½ teaspoon bicarbonate
  of soda (baking soda)
½ teaspoon baking
  powder
½ teaspoon sea salt flakes
130 g (4½ oz) unsalted
  butter, softened
200 g (7 oz) caster
  (superfine) sugar
50 g (1¾ oz) brown sugar
1 egg
2 teaspoons vanilla bean
  paste
1 teaspoon pistachio
  extract
70 g (2½ oz) slivered
  pistachios, roughly
  chopped
180 g (6 oz) dark chocolate
  (70%), roughly chopped
50 g (1¾ oz) dark chocolate
  chips, to garnish
30 g (1 oz) slivered
  pistachios, to garnish

Preheat the oven to 180°C (350°F) fan-forced. Line two baking trays with baking paper or silicone baking mats.

Using a food processor, grind the whole pistachios until they form a coarse meal.

Combine the ground pistachios, flour, bicarbonate of soda, baking powder and salt in a bowl. Give these dry ingredients a good whisk and set aside.

Using an electric mixer fitted with the paddle attachment, mix the butter, caster sugar and brown sugar for 2–3 minutes or until creamy. Add the egg, vanilla and pistachio extract and give a good mix to combine. Add the flour mixture, then mix in the chopped slivered pistachios and dark chocolate.

Divide the dough into 20 balls, using 70 g (2½ oz) dough for each one. Place on the baking trays, leaving plenty of room for spreading.

Bake the cookies for 15–17 minutes or until golden brown around the edges. To get your cookies perfectly round, see my tips on page 12. Garnish the warm cookies by scattering them with the chocolate chips and slivered pistachios. Allow the cookies to cool completely on the trays.

Earl Grey millionaire shortbread

Makes 14

Earl Grey pairs perfectly with caramel and dark chocolate. The floral tones together with the deep, dark, caramel notes and bitterness of the chocolate makes for a truly delicious and sophisticated shortbread. If Earl Grey isn't your jam, you can absolutely leave it out for a traditional millionaire shortbread, but give it a go – you may just surprise yourself.

110 g (3¾ oz) unsalted butter, softened
50 g (1¾ oz) caster (superfine) sugar
1 egg yolk
1 teaspoon vanilla bean paste
2 Earl Grey tea bags
140 g (5 oz) plain (all-purpose) flour
1 teaspoon baking powder
Pinch of salt
Gold leaf, to garnish

Caramel filling
120 ml (3¾ fl oz) thickened (whipping) cream
225 g (8 oz) caster (superfine) sugar
1 teaspoon salt
125 g (4½ oz) unsalted butter
1 teaspoon vanilla bean paste

Chocolate glaze
100 g (3½ oz) dark chocolate, chopped
60 g (2¼ oz) unsalted butter
1 tablespoon honey

Preheat the oven to 160°C (315°F) fan-forced. Line a 20 cm (8 inch) square cake tin with baking paper.

Using an electric mixer fitted with the paddle attachment, mix the butter, sugar, egg yolk and vanilla until light and fluffy. Open up the tea bags and tip the tea leaves into the bowl along with the flour, baking powder and salt. Mix until just combined, scraping down the side of the bowl to ensure there are no streaks of unmixed butter.

Press the dough into the cake tin in an even layer and bake for 20–25 minutes or until the shortbread is nicely golden brown and cooked through.

For the filling, pour the cream into a small saucepan and bring to a simmer.

Meanwhile, in a large saucepan, stir the sugar over medium heat until it has melted and begins to caramelise. (This is a dry caramel – i.e. there is no water – so you don't have to worry about it crystallising.) Continue stirring the caramel until it reaches a deep amber colour, then remove from the heat and carefully pour in the warm cream (it will splatter, which is why it's best to use a large saucepan). Once the cream is incorporated, add the salt, butter and vanilla. Return the caramel to the heat and cook until it reaches 118°C (244°F) on a sugar thermometer. This will ensure that your caramel sets and is sliceable.

Pour the caramel over the shortbread base and allow to cool completely at room temperature.

continued...

For the glaze, combine the chocolate, butter and honey in a microwave-safe bowl. Heat on medium in 30-second intervals, stirring in between, until completely melted.

Pour the glaze over the set caramel and spread it in an even layer. Place the slice in the fridge to chill completely.

Remove the slice from the tin and carefully cut it into 3 x 9 cm (1¼ x 3½ inch) bars. To get clean slices, heat up your knife by running it under hot water, then dry it. Clean the knife after each cut, repeating the heating and drying for every slice.

Garnish each bar with a little gold leaf (because we're extra fancy like that).

Miso dark chocolate flourless cookies

Makes 8
Gluten free

175 g (6 oz) icing
(confectioners') sugar
35 g (1¼ oz) dark cocoa
powder
50 g (1¾ oz) egg whites
2 teaspoons white miso
paste
150 g (5½ oz) dark
chocolate chips
1 teaspoon sea salt flakes

It took a lot of trial and error to get this recipe just right, but I felt it would be remiss to not include a gluten- and dairy-free cookie recipe in the Classy Gal chapter. Some brands of miso contain gluten, so if you need to keep these strictly gluten free and can't find a gluten-free miso paste, simply omit it. You can add a good whack of salt to bring some savoury balance.

Preheat the oven to 150°C (300°F) fan-forced. Line two baking trays with baking paper or silicone baking mats.

Combine the icing sugar and cocoa in a large bowl and whisk together to break down any lumps.

In a separate bowl, whisk the egg whites and miso paste together. (This helps break down the miso, making it easier to incorporate.) Add the miso mixture to the icing sugar and cocoa and mix into a thick, chocolate-brown batter. Fold in the chocolate chips.

Using a small cookie scoop, scoop balls of the batter onto the baking trays, leaving room for spreading. Sprinkle the balls with the salt flakes.

Bake the cookies for 14–15 minutes or until the tops are cracked and glossy (like a brownie). Allow them to cool completely on the trays – you may rip off the bottoms if you try to move them too soon. These guys are chewy and dense, almost erring on the side of a confectionery, and are best eaten on the day they're made.

Orange creams

Makes 23

These 'melt in your mouth' sandwich cookies are buttery and bright, with pops of fragrant orange zest and speckles of vanilla bean throughout. If you're not an orange fan, you can substitute it with the usual suspects: lemon, lime, grapefruit, mandarin or, if you can get your hands on it, fresh yuzu.

300 g (10½ oz) plain (all-purpose) flour, plus extra for dusting
½ teaspoon baking powder
½ teaspoon salt
110 g (3¾ oz) caster (superfine) sugar
Grated zest of 1 orange
165 g (5¾ oz) unsalted butter, softened
1 egg yolk
1 teaspoon vanilla bean paste

Orange cream
50 g (1¾ oz) unsalted butter, softened
150 g (5½ oz) icing (confectioners') sugar, plus extra for dusting
Juice of 1 orange
Pinch of citric acid (optional)

Combine the flour, baking powder and salt in a bowl. Give these dry ingredients a good whisk and set aside.

Using an electric mixer fitted with the paddle attachment, mix the caster sugar and orange zest on medium speed – this will help release the oils in the orange zest into the sugar, giving an even more vibrant flavour.

Add the butter, egg yolk and vanilla and mix until thoroughly combined but not aerated (we don't want these to spread in the oven). Finally, add the dry ingredients and mix until a soft dough forms.

Wrap the dough in plastic wrap and pop it in the fridge for 1–2 hours. This will ensure the biscuits don't spread in the oven.

Preheat the oven to 180°C (350°F) fan-forced. Line two baking trays with baking paper or silicone baking mats.

Roll out the dough on a lightly floured bench until 3–4 mm (⅛–³⁄₁₆ inch) thick. Use a fluted cutter to cut out 5 cm (2 inch) rounds and place them on the baking trays, leaving about 2.5 cm (1 inch) between each cookie for spreading.

Bake the cookies for 8–10 minutes or until they look dry all the way to the centre but are still blond. Allow them to cool for 10 minutes on the trays before transferring to a wire rack to cool completely.

For the orange cream, whisk the butter and icing sugar using the whisk attachment of the electric mixer for 3–4 minutes or until light and creamy. Gradually add the orange juice and whisk for 2–3 minutes or until emulsified. Finally, add the citric acid, if using, and mix to combine.

Transfer the orange cream to a piping bag fitted with a 1 cm (½ inch) round nozzle. Pipe 1 teaspoon of the cream into the centre of half the cookies and sandwich with the remaining cookies. Lightly dust the filled cookies with icing sugar.

Passionfruit curd macadamia thumbprints

Makes 16

Traditionally, thumbprints are made with a jam filling, as in my basic recipe on page 46. These have been levelled up with the inclusion of finely chopped macadamias and a passionfruit curd filling. Feel free to sub out the macadamias for desiccated coconut, almond meal or even chopped cashews.

Make the passionfruit curd a day ahead, if possible. It will keep in the fridge for up to 3 weeks.

120 g (4¼ oz) unsalted butter, softened
100 g (3½ oz) caster (superfine) sugar
1 egg yolk
1 teaspoon vanilla extract
180 g (6 oz) plain (all-purpose) flour
½ teaspoon baking powder
Pinch of salt
100 g (3½ oz) macadamias, finely chopped

Passionfruit curd
4 egg yolks
100 g (3½ oz) strained passionfruit pulp
75 g (2½ oz) caster (superfine) sugar
70 g (2½ oz) unsalted butter, cubed

For the passionfruit curd, combine the egg yolks, passionfruit pulp and sugar in a small saucepan. Stir constantly over low heat until the mixture has thickened enough to coat the back of the spoon. Remove from the heat and stir in the butter.

Transfer the passionfruit curd to a bowl, cover the surface with plastic wrap and place in the fridge to chill completely for at least 2 hours, but preferably overnight.

Line two baking trays with baking paper or silicone baking mats.

Using an electric mixer fitted with the paddle attachment, mix the butter, sugar, egg yolk and vanilla on medium speed until just combined – there's no need to aerate this mixture. Add the flour, baking powder and salt and mix on low speed until just combined.

Roll the dough into balls, using 25 g (1 oz) dough for each one, then roll them in the chopped macadamias before placing them on the baking trays. Using your thumb or the back of a measuring spoon, imprint a cavity into each ball. Pop the trays of cookies in the fridge for 30 minutes to chill (this will help them keep their shape during baking).

Meanwhile, preheat the oven to 180°C (350°F) fan-forced.

Bake the cookies for 10–12 minutes or until lightly golden brown. These will spread in the oven, so use my trick on page 12 to get them perfectly round. Allow the cookies to cool completely on the trays.

Fill the cavity of each cookie with 1 teaspoon of the passionfruit curd. (I just use a teaspoon here, but you may find it easier to use a piping bag.)

Passionfruit and chocolate sandwiches

Makes 16

When I was studying at uni, I had a part-time job at a chocolate shop. It was truly one of the best jobs of my life (you have no idea how much chocolate I consumed every shift) and it was there that I learned that making ganache does not have to be limited to cream and chocolate. You can use a fruit purée in place of the cream and the result is a bright, fruity and complex ganache. I've gone with passionfruit and dark chocolate, but other notable combinations include strawberry with milk chocolate, raspberry with dark chocolate, and mango with white chocolate.

Start the ganache a day ahead if you can, so it has plenty of time to chill and set.

150 g (5½ oz) unsalted butter, softened
100 g (3½ oz) caster (superfine) sugar
1 egg yolk
250 g (9 oz) plain (all-purpose) flour, plus extra for dusting
40 g (1½ oz) dark cocoa powder, plus extra to garnish
½ teaspoon salt

Passionfruit ganache
110 g (3¾ oz) strained passionfruit pulp
200 g (7 oz) dark chocolate, chopped
30 g (1 oz) unsalted butter, cubed

For the ganache, combine the strained passionfruit pulp, chopped chocolate and butter in a microwave-safe bowl. Heat on medium in 30-second intervals, stirring in between, until the chocolate is completely melted. If the ganache appears split, use a stick blender to emulsify it until smooth and glossy. Cover the surface of the ganache with plastic wrap and place it in the fridge until completely set for 2–3 hours (preferably overnight).

Preheat the oven to 160°C (315°F) fan-forced. Line two baking trays with baking paper or silicone baking mats.

Using an electric mixer fitted with the paddle attachment, mix the butter, sugar and egg yolk until combined, about 1–2 minutes (you don't need aeration here as you don't want the biscuits to spread in the oven). Add the flour, cocoa and salt and mix until just combined.

Roll out the dough on a lightly floured bench until 3–4 mm (⅛–³⁄₁₆ inch) thick. Use a ring cutter to cut 5 cm (2 inch) rounds and place them on the baking trays. If the dough is too soft to handle here, you can pop it into the fridge for 45–60 minutes to firm up.

Bake the cookies for 9–10 minutes or until they look dry all over. Allow them to cool for 10 minutes on the trays before transferring to a wire rack to cool completely.

Transfer the set ganache to a piping bag fitted with a French star tip. Pipe 1–2 teaspoons of the ganache onto half of the cookies and sandwich with the remaining cookies. Garnish by dusting half of each cookie with cocoa powder.

Bounty™ macarons

Makes 25
Gluten free

There is nothing quite like a freshly baked macaron – forget everything you thought you knew about store-bought macs (which have most likely been frozen for a while) and fall in love with these little French treats all over again. Most people I've spoken to are wildly intimidated by making macs at home but once you've done it a couple of times and know what you're looking for, they're not that complicated. The real pain point of these guys is the macaronage – folding the dry ingredients into the meringue. To make this a little easier, we're using a cooked Swiss meringue, which adds some stability to the macaronage and makes it harder to overwork the batter.

Start making the ganache a day ahead if you can, to allow plenty of time for it to chill and set.

130 g (4½ oz) almond meal
120 g (4¼ oz) icing (confectioners') sugar
20 g (¾ oz) dark cocoa powder
100 g (3½ oz) egg whites
90 g (3¼ oz) caster (superfine) sugar
80 g (2¾ oz) desiccated coconut, toasted (see page 126), to garnish

Chocolate coconut ganache
200 g (7 oz) milk chocolate, chopped
150 g (5½ oz) coconut cream
40 g (1½ oz) unsalted butter
¼ teaspoon coconut extract

For the ganache, combine the chocolate, coconut cream, butter and coconut extract in a microwave-safe bowl. Heat on medium in 30-second intervals, stirring in between, until completely melted. Stir the ganache until smooth and glossy, then cover the surface with plastic wrap and place in the fridge until completely set (preferably overnight).

Sift the almond meal, icing sugar and cocoa to combine. If your almond meal is a little coarse, you may need to blend it in a food processor in order to get smooth-topped macarons.

Combine the egg whites and caster sugar in the heatproof bowl of an electric mixer. Sit the bowl over a saucepan of simmering water, ensuring the bowl doesn't touch the water. Cook, stirring constantly, until the mixture reaches 70°C (158°F) on a sugar thermometer. (If you rub the mixture between two fingers, you shouldn't be able to feel any sugar crystals.)

Use the whisk attachment of the mixer to whisk the mixture on medium–high speed until a thick, glossy meringue forms.

Add the sifted dry ingredients and begin folding with a spatula. The aim here is to achieve a 'ribbon' consistency (when you pick up the spatula, the mixture should flow off it like a ribbon).

Transfer the mixture to a piping bag fitted with a 1 cm (½ inch) round nozzle. Line two baking trays with baking paper or silicone baking mats.

Pipe the macaron mixture into 3 cm (1¼ inch) rounds, allowing room for them to spread. Tap the trays on the bench two or three times to release any air bubbles trapped in the macaron shells (this also helps the shells to spread and flatten).

Allow the shells to sit at room temperature for 30–60 minutes or until a skin has formed on the surface.

Meanwhile, preheat the oven to 130°C (250°F) fan-forced.

Bake the macaron shells for 15–18 minutes. To test that they're ready, place a finger on top of a shell and try to move it – if it wobbles, it will need another 2–3 minutes in the oven. Allow the macarons to cool completely on the trays before attempting to move them; if you move them too soon, you risk the bottom of the macs tearing off.

Transfer the set ganache to a piping bag fitted with a 1 cm (½ inch) round nozzle. Pipe 2 teaspoons of the ganache into the centre of half the macaron shells and sandwich with the remaining shells. Roll the edges of the ganache in the toasted coconut on a plate.

Pictured overleaf

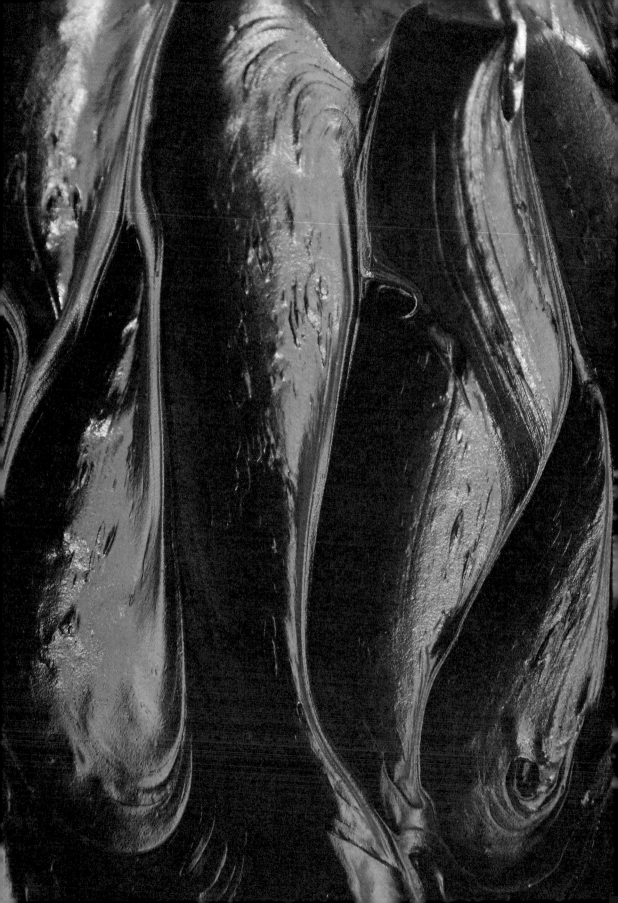

Mango and green tea macarons

Makes 25
Gluten free

I could have added some plain old macs here: a classic salted caramel, raspberry or vanilla. But with all my recipes, I like to encourage you to think outside the box when it comes to flavours. There is so much out there that can be transformed into impressive little bite-sized treats and the macaron is the perfect vehicle to experiment with flavours.

To get the most flavour out of the mango ganache, use the ripest mango you can find. If you're going to use frozen mango, make sure you defrost the mango first and drain off any liquid before puréeing to ensure you get the right set on the ganache. It's best to make the ganache a day ahead so it can chill and set overnight before you fill the macaron shells.

140 g (5 oz) almond meal
130 g (4½ oz) icing
   (confectioners') sugar
5 g (⅛ oz) matcha green
   tea powder
100 g (3½ oz) egg whites
90 g (3¼ oz) caster
   (superfine) sugar

Mango ganache
150 g (5½ oz) white
   chocolate, chopped
30 ml (1 fl oz) thickened
   (whipping) cream
60 g (2¼ oz) ripe mango,
   puréed
15 g (½ oz) unsalted butter

For the ganache, combine the white chocolate and cream in a microwave-safe bowl. Heat on medium in 30-second intervals, stirring in between, until the chocolate has completely melted. Stir in the mango purée and butter, then cover the surface with plastic wrap and place the ganache in the fridge until completely set (preferably overnight).

Sift the almond meal, icing sugar and matcha to combine. If your almond meal is a little coarse, you may need to blend it in a food processor in order to get smooth-topped macarons.

Combine the egg whites and caster sugar in the heatproof bowl of an electric mixer. Sit the bowl over a saucepan of simmering water, ensuring the bowl doesn't touch the water. Cook, stirring constantly, until the mixture reaches 70°C (158°F) on a sugar thermometer. (If you rub the mixture between two fingers, you shouldn't be able to feel any sugar crystals.)

Use the whisk attachment of the mixer to whisk the mixture on medium–high speed until a thick, glossy meringue forms.

Add the sifted dry ingredients and begin folding with a spatula. The aim here is to achieve a 'ribbon' consistency (when you pick up the spatula, the mixture should flow off it like a ribbon).

Transfer the mixture to a piping bag fitted with a 1 cm (½ inch) round nozzle. Line two baking trays with baking paper or silicone baking mats.

Pipe the macaron mixture into 3 cm (1¼ inch) rounds, allowing room for them to spread. Tap the trays on the bench two or three times to release any air bubbles trapped in the macaron shells (this also helps the shells to spread and flatten).

Allow the shells to sit at room temperature for 30–60 minutes or until a skin has formed on the surface.

Meanwhile, preheat the oven to 130°C (250°F) fan-forced.

Bake the macaron shells for 15–18 minutes. To test that they're ready, place a finger on top of a shell and try to move it – if it wobbles, it will need another 2–3 minutes in the oven. Allow the macarons to cool completely on the trays before attempting to move them; if you move them too soon, you risk the bottom of the macs tearing off.

Transfer the set ganache to a piping bag fitted with a 1 cm (½ inch) round nozzle. Pipe 1–2 teaspoons of the ganache into the centre of half the macaron shells and sandwich with the remaining shells.

Pictured overleaf

Raspberry parfait macaron sandwiches

Makes 25
Gluten free

Macaron shells make the perfect 'bread' for an ice-cream sandwich. Here I've used an easy, no-churn parfait recipe set as a slab and cut into rounds the same size as the macaron shells. When colouring macaron shells, never use an oil-based colour as the meringue won't whip. It's also good to note that the colour will lighten as the meringue aerates.

It's best to make the parfait a day ahead and freeze it overnight.

140 g (5 oz) almond meal
130 g (4½ oz) icing
  (confectioner's) sugar
100 g (3½ oz) egg whites
90 g (3¼ oz) caster
  (superfine) sugar
Red gel food colouring

Raspberry parfait
4 egg yolks
90 g (3¼ oz) caster
  (superfine) sugar
125 g (4½ oz) fresh
  raspberries, puréed
400 ml (14 fl oz) thickened
  (whipping) cream,
  whipped

For the parfait, combine the egg yolks and sugar in a heatproof bowl set over a saucepan of simmering water, ensuring the bowl doesn't touch the water. Whisk constantly (a hand-held electric mixer will save you some pain!) until the mixture is aerated and the sugar has dissolved (test by rubbing it between your fingers).

Fold in the raspberry purée and allow the mixture to cool completely, then fold in the whipped cream.

Pour the mixture into a 20 cm (8 inch) square cake tin lined with baking paper and freeze until completely set (overnight is best).

Sift the almond meal and icing sugar to combine. If your almond meal is a little coarse, you may need to blend it in a food processor in order to get smooth-topped macarons.

Combine the egg whites and caster sugar in the heatproof bowl of an electric mixer. Sit the bowl over a saucepan of simmering water, ensuring the bowl doesn't touch the water. Cook, stirring constantly, until the mixture reaches 70°C (158°F) on a sugar thermometer. (If you rub the mixture between two fingers, you shouldn't be able to feel any sugar crystals.)

Use the whisk attachment of the mixer to whisk the mixture on medium–high speed until a thick, glossy meringue forms.

Add the sifted dry ingredients and begin folding with a spatula. The aim here is to achieve a 'ribbon' consistency (when you pick up the spatula, the mixture should flow off it like a ribbon).

Transfer the mixture to a piping bag fitted with a 1 cm (½ inch) round nozzle. Line two baking trays with baking paper or silicone baking mats.

Pipe the macaron mixture into 3 cm (1¼ inch) rounds, allowing room for them to spread. Tap the trays on the bench two or three times to release any air bubbles trapped in the macaron shells (this also helps the shells to spread and flatten).

Allow the shells to sit at room temperature for 30–60 minutes or until a skin has formed on the surface.

Meanwhile, preheat the oven to 130°C (250°F) fan-forced.

Bake the macaron shells for 15–18 minutes. To test that they're ready, place a finger on top of a shell and try to move it – if it wobbles, it will need another 2–3 minutes in the oven. Allow the macarons to cool completely on the trays before attempting to move them; if you move them too soon, you risk the bottom of the macs tearing off.

To assemble, use a cookie cutter the same size as the macaron shells to cut out rounds of parfait. Sandwich the parfait rounds between two macaron shells. Place the parfait sandwiches in the freezer until you're ready to serve them. They can be frozen for 2–3 weeks. (Any left-over parfait can be frozen for up to 6 weeks.)

Pictured overleaf

Cinnamon, coffee and macadamia biscotti

Makes 20

Biscotti are a twice-baked biscuit that originally came from Italy and was made with almonds, which grow abundantly there. They are crunchy, nutty and perfect dipped in a cup of tea or coffee.

150 g (5½ oz) macadamias
170 g (5¾ oz) plain (all-purpose) flour
1 teaspoon bicarbonate of soda (baking soda)
1 teaspoon baking powder
½ teaspoon salt
2 eggs, at room temperature
2 tablespoons instant coffee powder
2 teaspoons ground cinnamon
120 g (4¼ oz) caster (superfine) sugar
1 tablespoon vanilla bean paste
200 g (7 oz) dark chocolate, melted

Preheat the oven to 170°C (325°F) fan-forced. Line two baking trays with baking paper or silicone baking mats.

Spread the macadamias on one of the baking trays and roast for 10–12 minutes or until lightly golden brown. Be careful not to burn them; you may need to stir them around halfway through to ensure they are evenly browned. Allow the nuts to cool and then roughly chop them – you want large chunks throughout the biscotti, so don't go too fine here.

Combine the flour, bicarbonate of soda, baking powder and salt in a bowl. Give these dry ingredients a good whisk and set aside.

Either by hand or using an electric mixer, mix the eggs, coffee powder, cinnamon, sugar and vanilla in a bowl until frothy – you don't need to aerate this, just loosen up the eggs and help the coffee to dissolve. Add the flour mixture and mix until a soft dough forms. Add the chopped macadamias (you might want to use your hands). The dough will be quite wet, but avoid adding extra flour as this will result in dry, tooth-breaking biscotti.

Tip the dough out onto one of the baking trays and, using a spatula, press it into a 30 cm (12 inch) log. I like to press the log so it's quite flat, around 2 cm (¾ inch) tall. The dough will rise in the oven and biscotti should be more on the thin side when sliced. Again, since the dough is quite wet, it won't be a perfect log, but don't be tempted to add any extra flour.

Bake the log for 35 minutes or until golden brown and puffy. Allow it to cool for 10 minutes.

Reduce the oven temperature to 140°C (275°F). Using a serrated knife, cut the log into 2 cm (¾ inch) slices. Place the biscotti on the baking trays and bake for 12–14 minutes, then flip them over and bake for another 10–12 minutes. Allow them to cool completely on the trays.

Dip one end of each biscotti into the melted chocolate. You can let the chocolate set at room temperature or place the biscotti in the fridge for 10–15 minutes to harden.

Apricot pistachio crumble bars

Makes 16

We all know that apricot and pistachios are a match made in heaven, and these pie-like bars don't disappoint. Make these bars in the heat of summer, when apricots are at their sweet, juicy best, perfectly complemented by the warm hum of the cardamom. The best part, though? We use the pistachio crust as a crumble for two separate textures, without having to make a separate streusel topping.

Pistachio crust

180 g (6 oz) plain (all-purpose) flour
110 g (3¾ oz) brown sugar
125 g (4½ oz) pistachios, finely chopped
1½ teaspoons baking powder
1 teaspoon ground cardamom
125 g (4½ oz) unsalted butter, cubed
Icing (confectioners') sugar, for dusting

Apricot filling

10 apricots, quartered
125 g (4½ oz) good-quality apricot jam
50 g (1¾ oz) caster (superfine) sugar
10 g (¼ oz) cornflour (cornstarch)
1 vanilla bean, seeds scraped

Start by making the pistachio crust. Preheat the oven to 180°C (350°F) fan-forced. Line a 20 cm (8 inch) square cake tin with baking paper so that the paper overhangs the sides of the tin.

Combine the flour, brown sugar, pistachios, baking powder and cardamom in a bowl and mix well. Use your fingertips to rub the butter into the dry ingredients until the mixture looks sandy and the butter is completely dispersed throughout.

Press two-thirds of the pistachio mixture into the base of the cake tin, using the flat base of a glass to press it into an even layer. Set the remaining mixture aside in the fridge to use for the topping.

Bake the base layer for 15 minutes or until light golden brown.

Meanwhile, for the filling, mix the apricots, jam, caster sugar, cornflour and vanilla seeds in a large bowl. Spread the mixture evenly over the top of the cookie base. Crumble the reserved pistachio mixture over the filling.

Bake the slab for 20–25 minutes or until the topping is golden brown and the apricots have cooked down to be sweet and jammy. Remove from the oven and leave to cool completely in the tin.

Cut the cooled crumble into 16 squares before dusting with icing sugar.

Limoncello spritz bars

Makes 14

Enter the adults-only cookie. This one is based on one of my favourite summer drinks, the limoncello spritz, and one of my favourite Aussie bakery treats, the lemon coconut slice. The bars are made from a lemon-scented shortbread that's crushed and set into a slice, then topped with limoncello icing. You could absolutely replace the limoncello with lemon juice to make these kiddie friendly. But it's about time we baked treats just for us, don't you think? Another great substitution: Aperol with orange. Dreamy.

250 g (9 oz) crushed lemon shortbread crumbs (see below)

200 g (7 oz) sweetened condensed milk

80 g (2¾ oz) unsalted butter, melted

100 g (3½ oz) desiccated coconut

Lemon coconut shortbread

90 g (3¼ oz) unsalted butter, softened

45 g (1½ oz) caster (superfine) sugar

1 egg yolk

Pinch of salt

Grated zest and juice of 1 lemon

140 g (5 oz) plain (all-purpose) flour

20 g (¾ oz) desiccated coconut

Limoncello icing

300 g (10½ oz) icing (confectioners') sugar

50 g (1¾ oz) unsalted butter, softened

50 ml (1¾ fl oz) limoncello

Preheat the oven to 170°C (325°F) fan-forced. Line a baking tray with baking paper or silicone baking mats, and line a 20 cm (8 inch) square cake tin with baking paper.

Start by making the lemon coconut shortbread. Using an electric mixer fitted with the paddle attachment, mix the butter, caster sugar, egg yolk and salt until smooth. You don't need to aerate this mixture, just get it nicely combined. Add the lemon zest, lemon juice, flour and coconut and mix until just combined.

Best part about this shortbread? No rolling out or cutting out shapes! Just press the dough onto the baking tray and bake for 25–30 minutes or until golden brown. Allow the shortbread to cool.

Crush the shortbread with your hands – I like to keep a few larger pieces in there for texture, but you can also use a food processor to blitz it to breadcrumb consistency.

Transfer 250 g (9 oz) of the shortbread crumbs to a bowl and add the condensed milk, melted butter and coconut. Mix to combine, then press the mixture into the cake tin in an even layer. Place in the fridge while you prepare the icing.

For the icing, combine the icing sugar, butter and limoncello in a bowl and whisk until completely smooth. The icing should be thick and spreadable.

Spread the icing over the shortbread base and return it to the fridge to set completely – overnight is best, but 1–2 hours should also do the job.

Cut the chilled slab into 3 x 9 cm (1¼ x 3½ inch) bars.

Kingston™ biscuits

Makes 20

Something I never really picked up on during all my years of eating Kingstons is that they are just little Anzac biscuits, dressed up with a touch of milk chocolate. Is that a bad thing? Considering Anzacs are one of the world's best bikkies (and for good reason), I think not. I've played around with the quantities of the ingredients from my original Anzac recipe (page 52) to get a more rounded cookie, with less spread.

145 g (5 oz) unsalted butter, softened
150 g (5½ oz) caster (superfine) sugar
45 g (1½ oz) golden syrup or honey
½ teaspoon bicarbonate of soda (baking soda)
120 g (4¼ oz) plain (all-purpose) flour
90 g (3¼ oz) rolled oats
60 g (2¼ oz) desiccated coconut
½ teaspoon salt
200 g (7 oz) milk chocolate

Preheat the oven to 170°C (325°F) fan-forced. Line two baking trays with baking paper or silicone baking mats.

Combine the butter, sugar and golden syrup or honey in a saucepan. Cook over medium heat until completely melted. Stir in the bicarbonate of soda and allow the mixture to fizz. Add the flour, oats, coconut and salt and mix until a thick dough forms. Allow the mixture to cool for 10 minutes.

Roll the dough into small balls, using 10–15 g (¼–½ oz) dough for each, and place on the baking trays, leaving room for them to spread slightly.

Bake the biscuits for 9–10 minutes or until golden brown. Allow them to cool for 10 minutes on the baking trays before transferring to a wire rack to cool completely.

Melt the chocolate, then allow it to sit at room temperature until it has begun to thicken up again – not so thick that you can't spoon it in between the biscuits, but not so thin that it just runs out when sandwiching.

Sandwich the biscuits with 1–2 teaspoons of the chocolate and allow it to set completely before eating.

Seed and nut cookies

Makes 14
Gluten free

These are a little riff on the Florentine, but instead of the faff of making a caramel to set the cookies, we are using egg white and sugar. The result? A light, mildly sweet, crispy cookie. Any mixture of seeds and nuts can be used – whatever you have on hand.

120 g (4¼ oz) sliced
  almonds
60 g (2¼ oz) pepitas
  (pumpkin seeds)
50 g (1¾ oz) sunflower
  seeds
1 tablespoon poppy seeds
2 egg whites
140 g (5 oz) icing
  (confectioners') sugar
½ teaspoon salt
100 g (3½ oz) white
  chocolate, tempered
  (see page 17)

Preheat the oven to 180°C (350°F) fan-forced. Line two baking trays with baking paper or silicone baking mats.

Spread the almonds, pepitas and sunflower seeds on one of the baking trays. Bake for 8–10 minutes or until golden brown. Allow to cool completely.

Reduce the oven temperature to 150°C (300°F).

Tip the cooled nut and seed mixture into a mixing bowl and add the poppy seeds, egg whites, icing sugar and salt. Mix until well combined.

Place a 6 cm (2½ inch) ring cutter on one of the baking trays. Take 1 tablespoon of the seed mixture and press it neatly into the ring, then remove the cutter. Repeat with the remaining seed mixture to make 14 rounds in total.

Bake the cookies for 30–35 minutes, then turn off the oven and allow them to cool completely in the oven (this will ensure they stay crisp when you store them). If any liquid leaches out and caramelises around the base of the cookies, simply trim it off with a ring cutter before the cookies cool.

Place the tempered white chocolate in a piping bag and snip off a small tip. Run the piping bag back and forth over the top of the cookies to create decorative lines. Allow the cookies to set at room temperature.

Chai-spiced sugar cookies

Makes 14

I absolutely adore chai, from the sugary pre-mixed drink to the proper double-boiled, loose-leaf chai with fresh spices and lots of peppercorns. What can I say? I'm a warm spice gal! I also love chai spices in baking. They work perfectly when combined with sugar and butter.

300 g (10½ oz) plain (all-purpose) flour, plus extra for dusting
½ teaspoon ground cardamom
½ teaspoon ground nutmeg
1 teaspoon ground cinnamon
½ teaspoon ground cloves
1½ teaspoons ground ginger
½ teaspoon ground black peppercorns
½ teaspoon salt
170 g (5¾ oz) unsalted butter, softened
140 g (5 oz) caster (superfine) sugar
1 egg
1 teaspoon vanilla bean paste
150 g (5½ oz) white chocolate, tempered (see page 17)
Dried rose petals and gold leaf, to garnish

Combine the flour, spices and salt in a bowl and whisk together to evenly disperse the spices and break down any lumps.

Using an electric mixer fitted with the paddle attachment, cream the butter and sugar. You aren't looking for this to be light and fluffy, just a cohesive mixture. Add the egg and vanilla and mix to combine. Scrape down the side of the bowl to ensure there are no large streaks of butter that will affect the final cookies. Add the flour mixture and mix until just combined.

Divide the dough in half and wrap each piece in plastic wrap. Refrigerate the dough for 1–2 hours (or overnight if you have time). This will help prevent the cookies from spreading during baking.

Preheat the oven to 170°C (325°F) fan-forced. Line two baking trays with baking paper or silicone baking mats.

Roll out the dough on a lightly floured bench until about 1 cm (½ inch) thick, stopping and rotating as you go to ensure it isn't sticking to the bench (and adding small amounts of flour if it is). Use a fluted cutter to cut out 6 cm (2½ inch) rounds and place them on the baking trays.

Bake the cookies for 14–16 minutes or until golden brown around the edges. Allow them to cool for 5 minutes on the trays before transferring to a wire rack to cool completely.

I like to drizzle these with tempered white chocolate and sprinkle them with dried rose petals and gold leaf. Totally optional!

Monte Carlo™ biscuits

Makes 16

The Monte Carlo is an Australian institution. It was always first to disappear when a packet of Arnott's Assorted Cream biscuits was opened for morning tea, closely followed by the Kingston (page 172).

150 g (5½ oz) unsalted butter, softened
150 g (5½ oz) caster (superfine) sugar
1 teaspoon vanilla extract
40 g (1½ oz) golden syrup or honey
1 egg
50 g (1¾ oz) desiccated coconut
260 g (9¼ oz) plain (all-purpose) flour
2-3 tablespoons good-quality raspberry jam

American buttercream
70 g (2½ oz) unsalted butter, softened
175 g (6 oz) icing (confectioners') sugar
1 tablespoon milk

Using an electric mixer fitted with the paddle attachment, mix the butter, caster sugar, vanilla and golden syrup or honey until well combined – no need to aerate, just mix until smooth before adding the egg and giving a further mix until cohesive. Add the coconut and flour and mix until the dough just comes together.

Turn the dough out onto a long piece of plastic wrap and wrap tightly to form a log. I like to try to get a slight oval shape here to make the biscuits look as authentic as possible. Refrigerate the dough for 30–60 minutes.

Preheat the oven to 180°C (350°F) fan-forced. Line two baking trays with baking paper or silicone baking mats.

Cut the chilled dough into 1 cm (½ inch) thick slices and place on the baking trays.

Bake for 15–17 minutes or until the cookies are golden brown. Allow them to cool for 10 minutes on the baking trays before transferring to a wire rack to cool completely.

For the buttercream, combine the butter and icing sugar in the bowl of an electric mixer fitted with the paddle attachment and mix until smooth. Add the milk and mix again until combined. Transfer the buttercream to a piping bag and snip off a small tip. (You can also use a spoon to dollop the buttercream.)

Spread ½ teaspoon of the raspberry jam onto the cookies, then pipe or dollop 2 teaspoons of the buttercream on top of half the cookies and sandwich with the remaining cookies. I like to pop these in the fridge for 30 minutes for the buttercream to firm up before eating. Nostalgia at its best.

Almond and coconut chocolate clusters

Makes 15
Gluten free

If we call these a no-bake cookie, then they technically qualify for inclusion in this book. Let's be honest, though, these are a chocolate, not a cookie, but I desperately wanted to include them because they are wildly delicious and that's what this cookie book is all about. The other great things about them are that they are super simple to make and perfect for gifting. You can use any type of nut that you love, and leave out the coconut if you prefer. And you can swap the dark chocolate with milk, white, golden or ruby.

150 g (5½ oz) slivered almonds
60 g (2¼ oz) shredded coconut
80 g (2¾ oz) caster (superfine) sugar
Pinch of salt
250 g (9 oz) dark chocolate, melted

Preheat the oven to 160°C (315°F) fan-forced. Line a baking tray with baking paper or a silicone baking mat.

Spread the almonds and coconut on the tray and bake for 6–8 minutes or until lightly golden brown.

Combine the sugar and 50 ml (1¾ fl oz) water in a small saucepan. Bring to the boil over medium heat and cook until the mixture reaches 116°C (241°F) on a sugar thermometer, then stir in the toasted almonds and coconut and the salt. The sugar should crystallise on the nuts, making the mixture appear white and sandy.

Spread the caramelised nuts on the baking tray and allow them to cool completely.

Stir the caramelised nuts through the melted chocolate. Spoon the mixture back onto the baking tray to set, using 1 tablespoon of the mixture for each cluster. You can speed up the setting process by placing the clusters in the fridge, or just leave them to set at room temperature.

Persian love cookies

Makes 18
Gluten free

If you haven't been lucky enough to enjoy a big slice of Persian love cake, then I strongly suggest that you try it (the recipe can be found in my first book). It's floral, fragrant, nutty and just delicious. These cookies tick all of those boxes: classy little flavour-packed morsels that are so easy to put together.

120 g (4¼ oz) almond meal
130 g (4½ oz) pistachio meal
130 g (4½ oz) caster (superfine) sugar
3 egg whites
1 teaspoon rosewater
1 teaspoon ground cardamom
5 g (⅛ oz) dried rose petals
100 g (3½ oz) slivered pistachios

Preheat the oven to 140°C (275°F) fan-forced. Line two baking trays with baking paper or silicone baking mats.

Combine the almond meal, pistachio meal and sugar in a bowl and set aside.

In a separate bowl, whisk two of the egg whites until they begin to foam – you don't need to go for stiff peaks here but if you do, you'll end up with a beautiful rustic cracked cookie (which I love!). Fold in the almond meal mixture along with the rosewater, cardamom and dried rose petals.

Tip the slivered pistachios onto a plate. Lightly whisk the remaining egg white to break it up.

Roll 25 g (1 oz) of the dough into a ball, then dip it in the egg white before rolling it in the slivered pistachios to coat. Place the ball on one of the trays and repeat with the remaining dough.

Bake the cookies for 18–20 minutes or until beginning to turn golden brown at the edges. Allow them to cool completely on the trays.

The
World
Traveller

Spiced plum and hazelnut Linzer cookies —— 188

Mahlepi Koulourakia —— 190

Cashew kourabiedes —— 193

Italian crostoli —— 194

Rugelach —— 196

German pfeffernüsse —— 198

Polish kolaczki —— 203

French cinnamon palmiers —— 204

Pizzelle della Nonna —— 206

Puerto Rican Besitos de Coco —— 209

German poppy-seed and marzipan cookies —— 210

Vanilice with plum jam —— 212

Speculoos cream stars —— 215

Double-chocolate peppermint cookies —— 216

Glazed gingerbread —— 218

Fruity meringue clouds —— 221

Almond toffee bark —— 222

Vaniljekranse —— 224

You may realise at this point that I am a serial feeder at heart. My love of baking comes from my personal love of sugar, yes, but I also find complete joy in sharing my bakes with those who mean the most to me. You could say it's my love language. This chapter is all about that: sharing the love with festive treats from around the globe. While I do really enjoy gifting things to people in general, I find it extra special to give a loved one something home-made, and what fits the bill better than cookies?

Spiced plum and hazelnut Linzer cookies

Makes 28

A Linzer cookie is a real thing of beauty: a delicate shortbread-like cookie, traditionally sandwiched with raspberry jam, but in this case, plum jam. I love how completely customisable these are – not a fan of hazelnuts? Swap them out for almond meal, or leave them out altogether. Not in the mood for jam? Try sandwiching these with chocolate hazelnut spread in place of the plum jam. You won't regret it.

You can make the dough a day or two in advance and let it rest in the fridge before rolling.

220 g (7¾ oz) unsalted butter, softened
150 g (5½ oz) icing (confectioners') sugar, plus extra for dusting
2 egg yolks
½ teaspoon fine salt
½ teaspoon ground cinnamon
¼ teaspoon ground nutmeg
½ teaspoon ground cloves
1 teaspoon vanilla bean paste
300 g (10½ oz) plain (all-purpose) flour
100 g (3½ oz) hazelnut meal
240 g (8½ oz) good-quality plum jam

Using an electric mixer fitted with the paddle attachment, cream the butter, icing sugar and egg yolks until light and fluffy. Add the salt, spices and vanilla and mix to combine, stopping and scraping down the side of the bowl and the paddle. Add the flour and hazelnut meal and mix until a soft dough forms.

Wrap the dough in plastic wrap and refrigerate for 2–3 hours (or up to a day or two) or until completely firm.

Preheat the oven to 160°C (315°F) fan-forced. Line two baking trays with baking paper or silicone baking mats.

Give the chilled dough a light knead until pliable. Divide the dough in half and roll out one half on a lightly floured bench until 3 mm (⅛ inch) thick. (This may seem quite thin, but remember that the cookies will be sandwiched together.) Cut out the cookie bases and place them on the baking trays. I've used fluted 6 cm (2½ inch) cutters, but since they're traditionally a Christmas treat, you could also use star or Christmas tree cookie cutters.

Bake the cookies for 12–15 minutes or until lightly golden around the edges. Allow them to cool on the trays for 10 minutes, then transfer to a wire rack to cool completely.

Meanwhile, roll out the remaining dough and cut out the cookie lids using the same cutter as for the bases, with a smaller cut-out in the middle. Place the cookie lids on the trays and bake, then cool as above.

Dust the cookie lids with icing sugar. Spread the cookies bases with 1–2 teaspoons of the plum jam and top with the lids.

Mahlepi Koulourakia

Makes 24

Traditionally a Greek Easter biscuit, these little twists are the perfect cookie for dipping into a cup of coffee. They're crisp on the outside, but soft and almost cake-like on the inside, and gently flavoured with orange and vanilla. You could add any flavourings you like to these. I've added mahlepi, a spice with a unique aroma and tones of almond and vanilla, but it's optional – look for it in delicatessens or specialty spice stores. Mastic, cinnamon or nutmeg would be great, too (I know, I know, totally non-traditional).

170 g (5¾ oz) unsalted butter, softened
160 g (5½ oz) caster (superfine) sugar
1 egg
Grated zest of 1 orange
1 tablespoon orange juice
1 tablespoon vanilla extract
1 tablespoon mahlepi powder
420 g (14¾ oz) plain (all-purpose) flour
¾ teaspoon baking powder
½ teaspoon bicarbonate of soda (baking soda)
2 egg yolks
40 g (1½ oz) sesame seeds

Preheat the oven to 160°C (315°F). Line two baking trays with baking paper or silicone baking mats.

Using an electric mixer fitted with the paddle attachment, mix the butter and sugar for 2–3 minutes until pale and fluffy. Add the egg, orange zest, orange juice, vanilla and mahlepi and mix to combine. The mixture may appear split at this stage, but it will come together when you mix in the flour.

Add the flour, baking powder and bicarbonate of soda and mix for 4–5 minutes or until the dough begins to peel away from the side of the bowl. The dough should be soft, but not sticky.

Take a 40 g (1½ oz) piece of dough and roll it into a 15 cm (6 inch) log. Fold the log in half and twist it around itself twice before placing it on one of the trays. Repeat with the remaining dough.

Whisk the egg yolks with 3 tablespoons water to make an egg wash. Brush the cookies with the egg wash and sprinkle with the sesame seeds.

Bake the cookies for 16–18 minutes or until lightly golden brown. Allow them to cool for 10 minutes before transferring to a wire rack to cool completely.

Cashew kourabiedes

Makes 24

I already know, as I am writing this, that I am going to receive a few angry emails about the illegitimacy of these kourabiedes. For the traditional version, see my first book. We are all about reinvention around these parts, and while the traditional almond type are flawless, there's nothing I love more than a perfectly roasted cashew. Slightly fattier than an almond, oilier and perfect with the tender kourabiedes dough.

225 g (8 oz) unsalted butter, softened

90 g (3¼ oz) icing (confectioners') sugar, plus extra for dusting

1 egg yolk

1 tablespoon milk

1 tablespoon vanilla bean paste

½ teaspoon ground cinnamon

340 g (11¾ oz) plain (all-purpose) flour, plus extra for dusting

¼ teaspoon baking powder

½ teaspoon salt

125 g (4½ oz) cashews, roasted and roughly chopped

Preheat the oven to 180°C (350°F) fan-forced. Line two baking trays with baking paper or silicone baking mats.

Using an electric mixer fitted with the paddle attachment, cream the butter and icing sugar until light and fluffy. This is the most important step of this recipe – you need to cream these for a good 8–10 minutes or until the butter is as pale as it can be. This will give you a lighter biscuit base.

Add the egg yolk, milk, vanilla and cinnamon and mix until combined. Add the flour, baking powder and salt along with the chopped cashews and mix together. The dough should be soft but not overly sticky.

Roll out the dough on a lightly floured bench until 1.5–2 cm (⅝–¾ inch) thick. Use a 7 cm (2¾ inch) ring cutter to cut one round of dough (this one won't be baked). Then, use the cutter to cut out a half-moon shape above the first round to create a beautiful C-shaped biscuit. Transfer the biscuit to one of the baking trays. Keep moving the cutter along the dough to cut out the remaining shapes.

Bake the biscuits for 16–18 minutes or until golden brown at the edges. Allow them to cool for 5–7 minutes (they should still be warm) before dusting liberally, and I mean liberally, with icing sugar. There's no overdoing the sugar here, so go for gold!

Italian crostoli

Makes 35

Crostoli is a delicacy, often gifted at Christmas. It originates from the Italian word 'storto', which means crooked or twisted. Given the appearance of these simple-yet-satisfying beauties, it's a suitable name. The dough is reminiscent of a pasta dough, spiked with grappa and sweetened slightly (which helps with caramelisation when frying). Fun fact: you can also use this dough to make cannoli.

165 g (5¾ oz) plain
   (all-purpose) flour,
   plus extra for dusting
1 egg
1 egg yolk
25 g (1 oz) caster
   (superfine) sugar
Grated zest of 1 lemon
10 g (¼ oz) unsalted butter,
   melted
1 tablespoon grappa
   (traditionally), rum
   or amaretto
Neutral-flavoured oil,
   such as canola or
   grapeseed, for frying
Icing (confectioners')
   sugar, for dusting

Using an electric mixer fitted with the paddle attachment, mix the flour, egg, egg yolk, caster sugar, lemon zest, butter and grappa until the dough comes together in a ball.

Wrap the dough in plastic wrap and allow it to rest at room temperature for 1–2 hours.

Divide the dough into six portions. Liberally dust each portion with flour before rolling it through a pasta machine. I usually stop after the second-thinnest setting of the machine. (You can use a rolling pin instead and roll the dough until it's 1–2 mm or about ⅟₁₆ inch thick.)

Cut the dough into 4 x 15 cm (1½ x 6 inch) strips and then cut a slit down the centre of each strip. Gently fold one side of the crostoli through the strip.

Heat the oil to 180°C (350°F) in a deep frying pan or saucepan. Fry the crostoli for 3–4 minutes or until golden brown. I like to only fry two or three crostoli at a time so they have plenty of room to puff up.

Drain the crostoli on a wire rack until completely cooled before liberally dusting them with icing sugar.

Rugelach

Makes 15

Little crescent-shaped pastries masquerading as cookies, these traditional Jewish delights are usually filled with sugar, nuts and fruits. I've used apricot jam and walnuts, but you could use whatever you love – chocolate hazelnut cream, plum jam with roasted chopped almonds, or even a grapefruit curd.

Start the dough a day ahead, if possible, so it has time to firm up before rolling.

125 g (4½ oz) unsalted butter, softened
100 g (3½ oz) cream cheese, at room temperature
40 g (1½ oz) caster (superfine) sugar
140 g (5 oz) plain (all-purpose) flour
½ teaspoon salt
50 g (1¾ oz) white (granulated) sugar
½ teaspoon ground cinnamon
100 ml (3½ fl oz) full-cream milk, for brushing

Filling
50 g (1¾ oz) caster (superfine) sugar
75 g (2½ oz) walnuts, finely chopped
25 g (1 oz) currants
½ teaspoon ground cinnamon
50 g (1¾ oz) good-quality apricot jam

Using an electric mixer fitted with the paddle attachment, mix the butter, cream cheese and caster sugar until smooth. Add the flour and salt and mix until a soft dough forms.

Wrap the dough in plastic wrap and press it into a rectangular shape. Refrigerate until firm (overnight is best).

Preheat the oven to 180°C (350°F) fan-forced. Line two baking trays with baking paper or silicone baking mats.

Divide the chilled dough into thirds. Return two of the pieces to the fridge while you work with the third. Roll out the dough into a large rectangle on a lightly floured bench until 3 mm (⅛ inch) thick – it should be roughly 25 x 15 cm (10 x 6 inches). Transfer to a baking tray and place in the fridge and repeat with the remaining dough.

To make the filling, mix the caster sugar, walnuts, currants and cinnamon together in a small bowl.

Working with one dough sheet at a time (leave the rest in the fridge), cut the dough into five triangles – picture a croissant, as you're aiming for a similar shape. If at any stage the dough gets too soft to work with, return it to the fridge for 15 minutes.

Spread one-third of the jam over the triangles and sprinkle with one-third of the walnut mixture. Roll up each triangle, starting from the longest side and finishing at the point. Shape the rolled-up dough into crescents on one of the trays and chill in the fridge for 30 minutes before baking. Repeat with the remaining dough, jam and filling.

Mix the white sugar and cinnamon in a small bowl. Brush the rugelach with the milk and sprinkle with the cinnamon sugar.

Bake the rugelach for 15–16 minutes or until lightly golden brown. Allow them to cool completely on the trays.

German pfeffernüsse

Makes 24

The process for making these beauties is three step, but super simple. A German alternative to the well-known gingerbread, these are made with a spice mix called 'lebkuchengewürz' (recipe below). Step one: make the spice mix. Step two: make the dough. Step three: bake and glaze. Simple! You'll find these floating around the supermarket shelves at Christmas time but, just like most baked goods, home-made is always extra special.

Start the dough a day ahead, if possible.

150 g (5½ oz) plain
  (all-purpose) flour
20 g (¾ oz) almond meal
1 teaspoon bicarbonate
  of soda (baking soda)
¼ teaspoon salt
¼ teaspoon ground white
  pepper
3 teaspoons
  lebkuchengewürz
  spice mix (see below)
60 g (2¼ oz) brown sugar
60 g (2¼ oz) honey
40 g (1½ oz) unsalted butter
1 egg yolk

Lebkuchengewürz

1 tablespoon ground
  cinnamon
1 teaspoon ground cloves
½ teaspoon ground allspice
½ teaspoon ground ginger
½ teaspoon ground nutmeg
½ teaspoon ground star
  anise
¼ teaspoon ground
  cardamom
¼ teaspoon ground
  coriander

For the lebkuchengewürz spice mix, simply combine all of the ingredients and mix well. Store it in an airtight container for 3–4 weeks.

Combine the flour, almond meal, bicarbonate of soda, salt, white pepper and 3 teaspoons of the spice mix in a bowl and mix well.

Meanwhile, in a small saucepan, combine the brown sugar, honey and butter and cook over low heat until the mixture has just melted together. Increase the heat and cook until the sugar has dissolved and the mixture comes to the boil. Remove from the heat and leave to cool for 5–10 minutes.

Pour the cooled wet ingredients into the dry ingredients, followed by the egg yolk, and stir until everything comes together in a soft dough.

Wrap the dough in plastic wrap and place in the fridge until completely chilled (overnight is best here, but you can also make the dough 2–3 days in advance).

Preheat the oven to 180°C (350°F) fan-forced. Line two baking trays with baking paper or silicone baking mats.

Divide the chilled dough into 15 g (½ oz) pieces and roll them into balls. Place the balls on the baking trays, leaving 3 cm (1¼ inches) between them.

Bake the biscuits for 12–14 minutes or until puffed up and lightly golden brown around the edges. Allow them to cool on the trays for 10 minutes before transferring to a wire rack to cool completely.

Glaze
300 g (10½ oz) icing (confectioners') sugar

Once the biscuits are cool, make the glaze. Put the icing sugar in a bowl with 3–4 tablespoons water and whisk until smooth. Dip the top of each pfeffernüsse into the glaze, then place it back on the wire rack to allow the excess to drip off.

Allow the glaze to dry completely (for about 30–60 minutes) before eating. These make a delicious tea-time treat or gift.

Pictured overleaf

Polish kolaczki

Makes 30

Kolaczki are a filled cookie made with a very similar dough to rugelach (page 196); they're both made with cream cheese and butter, which results in a light and flaky texture. These contain only a few ingredients and are quite straightforward – perfect for the busy Christmas period. This recipe makes quite a few, so I suggest using several different types of jam to make multiple flavours at the same time. I've used plum, raspberry and apricot.

120 g (4¼ oz) cream cheese, at room temperature
160 g (5½ oz) unsalted butter, softened
Pinch of salt
180 g (6 oz) plain (all-purpose) flour
White (granulated) sugar, for rolling
1 jar good-quality jam of your choice
1 egg white
Icing (confectioners') sugar, for dusting (optional)

Preheat the oven to 180°C (350°F) fan-forced. Line two baking trays with baking paper or silicone baking mats.

Using an electric mixer fitted with the paddle attachment, mix the cream cheese, butter and salt until smooth. Add the flour and mix until a soft dough forms.

Wrap the dough in plastic wrap and refrigerate for 1–2 hours or until firm enough to handle (you can do this the night before if you like).

Divide the dough in half for easier handling. Liberally sprinkle your work surface with white sugar. This will stop the cookies from sticking to the bench, but also add a nice sweet crunch to your bake. Roll out the dough until about 5 mm (¼ inch) thick.

Cut the dough into 5 cm (2 inch) squares – you can use a fluted roller to get cute edges here. Fill each square with ½ teaspoon of the jam. Fold the two outer corners together, brush the edge with a little egg white and press to seal.

Bake the kolaczki for 16 minutes or until lightly golden brown. Allow them to cool completely on the trays.

Serve as is, or dust with icing sugar.

French cinnamon palmiers

Makes 20

These French treats are traditionally made with puff pastry but that can be a little complex (read: intimidating) to make, so I've made your life substantially easier with rough puff pastry. Rough puff is much more of a throw-together situation, but my key piece of advice is to keep it chilled throughout all the steps.

250 g (9 oz) plain
(all-purpose) flour,
plus extra for dusting
Pinch of salt
250 g (9 oz) chilled
unsalted butter, cubed
125 ml (4 fl oz) iced water
50 g (1¾ oz) caster
(superfine) sugar
2 tablespoons ground
cinnamon

**Cinnamon sugar
sprinkle**
100 g (3½ oz) raw sugar
3 teaspoons ground
cinnamon

Combine the flour and salt in a bowl. Add the butter and use your fingertips to gently coat it with the flour. Try to keep the butter intact and don't rub it down too much – this is what is going to create the layers in the pastry.

Pour in the water and bring the mixture together into a rough dough. It will be quite crumbly, but just force it into a square and wrap it in plastic wrap. Refrigerate the dough for 30–40 minutes. This will ensure that the butter is completely chilled and help the dry flour to hydrate.

Roll out the pastry on a lightly floured bench into a long rectangle. Fold the pastry into three by folding one end to the middle, then the other end over the top, creating the first three layers. Refrigerate the pastry for 15–30 minutes.

Repeat this process three times, refrigerating the pastry each time to allow the gluten to relax and the butter to remain chilled (this helps create a flaky pastry). After the final folding step, chill the pastry for a further 1 hour before using.

Preheat the oven to 180°C (350°F) fan-forced. Line two baking trays with baking paper or silicone baking mats.

Cut the chilled pastry in half and roll it into a 45 x 25 cm (17½ x 10 inch) rectangle, about 5 mm (¼ inch) thick. Liberally sprinkle the pastry with the caster sugar and cinnamon before rolling up one end to the centre of the rectangle, followed by the second end so the two ends meet. This will give you the classic palmier shape. (At this stage, if the dough feels a little soft, you can wrap it up and refrigerate it again.) Slice the dough into 1 cm (½ inch) slices and lay them on the baking tray.

Make the cinnamon sugar sprinkle by combining the raw sugar and cinnamon. Sprinkle this over the dough slices.

Bake the palmiers for 18–20 minutes or until deep golden brown and caramelised. Allow them to cool completely on the trays.

Pizzelle della Nonna

Makes 10

Essentially a gorgeous little Christmas-time waffle, these delicate cookies get their form from a special pizzelle iron. A thick batter is dropped into the iron, which is placed over the stove to create the thin, snappy and beautifully patterned treats. It really is worth hunting down a pizzelle iron so you can make these yourself – try a specialty kitchenware store or look online. You can also use a shallow waffle iron.

160 g (5½ oz) plain (all-purpose) flour
90 g (3¼ oz) caster (superfine) sugar
½ teaspoon baking powder
¼ teaspoon salt
3 eggs
30 ml (1 fl oz) neutral-flavoured oil, such as rice bran oil
1 teaspoon vanilla bean paste
¼ teaspoon almond, anise or rum extract (optional)

Whisk the flour, sugar, baking powder and salt in a large mixing bowl until well combined.

In a separate bowl, combine the eggs, oil, vanilla and extract, if using, and whisk until smooth. Slowly add this mixture to the flour mixture, whisking to remove any lumps. Once the batter is smooth, it's time to cook.

Preheat a pizzelle iron or a shallow waffle iron.

Place a tablespoon of the batter into the centre of the iron and close the iron. Cook over medium heat until the cookie is a light golden brown.

These are traditionally served flat, but you can roll them up while they're still hot and flexible, then leave them to cool. You can also dress the pizzelle up by sandwiching them with melted chocolate or a chocolate hazelnut spread (such as Nutella).

Puerto Rican Besitos de Coco

Makes 18

Much like a coconut macaroon in flavour and texture, these Puerto Rican coconut kisses flip the ingredients on their head, using the egg yolks in place of the egg whites that macaroons use. They're a festive staple in South America and for good reason: easy to make, delicious to eat and perfect for gifting.

4 egg yolks
150 g (5½ oz) brown sugar
50 g (1¾ oz) unsalted
  butter, softened
1 tablespoon vanilla extract
1 teaspoon coconut extract
200 g (7 oz) shredded
  coconut
70 g (2½ oz) plain
  (all-purpose) flour
200 g (7 oz) dark
  chocolate, melted

Preheat the oven to 180°C (350°F) fan-forced. Line two baking trays with baking paper or silicone baking mats.

Combine the egg yolks, brown sugar and butter in a large bowl and mix by hand or using an electric mixer until just combined. Add the vanilla and coconut extracts and mix well to ensure they are evenly dispersed throughout the mixture. Add the shredded coconut and flour and mix to combine.

Scoop the mixture into balls, using 30 g (1 oz) for each one. Place the balls on the baking trays, leaving 2.5 cm (1 inch) between each one.

Bake the cookies for 14–15 minutes or until golden brown. Allow them to cool for 10 minutes before transferring to a wire rack to cool completely.

I like to coat the cookie bases in chocolate and then decorate the tops. Put the chocolate in a piping bag, snip off a small tip and then pipe about 1 teaspoon onto the base of the cookies. I press the cookies back onto the paper-lined trays, which means they set nice and flat. Pipe the remaining chocolate back and forth over the tops of the cookies. Allow the chocolate to set before eating.

German poppy-seed and marzipan cookies

Makes 18

These delicate little shortbread cookies – spritzgebäck – are a German Christmas classic. Marzipan is an almond paste that adds a beautiful softness and moisture to your bakes as well as adding a rich almond flavour. I've included instructions for making your own marzipan, but you can buy this if you prefer. Home-made marzipan can be stored in the fridge for up to 2 weeks or frozen for 3–4 months. You can also prepare the cookie dough a day or two in advance and store it in the fridge until you're ready to roll it out.

350 g (12 oz) marzipan (see below)
240 g (8½ oz) unsalted butter, softened
100 g (3½ oz) icing (confectioners') sugar, plus extra for dusting
1 teaspoon vanilla extract
1 teaspoon almond extract
½ teaspoon salt
1 egg
325 g (11½ oz) plain (all-purpose) flour
40 g (1½ oz) cornflour (cornstarch)
100 g (3½ oz) poppy seeds
100 g (3½ oz) good-quality plum jam

Marzipan
270 g (9½ oz) almond meal
210 g (7½ oz) icing (confectioners') sugar
2 teaspoons almond extract

To make the marzipan, blend the almond meal, icing sugar, almond extract and 60 ml (2 fl oz) water in a food processor until a soft dough forms. Shape the dough into a log, then tightly wrap it in plastic wrap and place it in the fridge until needed.

Using an electric mixer fitted with the paddle attachment, mix 100 g (3½ oz) of the marzipan with the butter and icing sugar on medium speed until smooth and homogenous. Add the vanilla and almond extracts, salt and egg and mix until just combined. Add the flour, cornflour and poppy seeds and mix until a soft dough forms.

Wrap the dough in plastic wrap and refrigerate for 2–3 hours or until firm.

Preheat the oven to 160°C (315°F) fan-forced. Line two baking trays with baking paper or silicone baking mats.

Divide the dough in half. Roll out each half on a lightly floured bench until 4–5 mm (³⁄₁₆–¼ inch) thick. Use a fluted cutter to cut out 7 cm (2¾ inch) rounds and place them on the baking trays.

Bake the cookies for 16–17 minutes or until very lightly golden brown. Allow them to cool for 10 minutes on the trays before transferring to a wire rack to cool completely.

Lightly dust your bench with icing sugar and roll out the remaining marzipan until 2 mm (¹⁄₁₆ inch) thick. Use the same fluted cutter to cut out discs of marzipan. Spoon ¼ teaspoon of the plum jam onto the cookies. Top half of the cookies with a marzipan disc and sandwich with the remaining cookies. Dust with icing sugar before serving.

Vanilice with plum jam

Makes 20

My baba was an incredible baker and she made these biscuits all the time. I never got the actual recipe from her, although the recipe might not have been much use as my grandmother always used random cups and hand measurements, and her recipes were closely guarded secrets. I don't know if vanilice were the exact cookie that she made; hers certainly seemed a little cakier. However, I do know that I LOVED the ones she made. I ate, and ate, and ate and ate them, every time she made them. Traditionally, these are made with either apricot or rosehip jam, but my baba had plum trees and so plum jam was a cornerstone of my childhood.

I like to roast the walnuts for extra-toasty flavour before grinding them, but you can skip this step if you like.

125 g (4½ oz) walnuts
125 g (4½ oz) unsalted
  butter, softened
130 g (4½ oz) caster
  (superfine) sugar
1 egg
1 tablespoon vanilla
  bean paste
½ teaspoon salt
325 g (11½ oz) plain
  (all-purpose) flour
1 jar good-quality
  plum jam
Icing (confectioners')
  sugar, for dusting

Preheat the oven to 180°C (350°F) fan-forced. Line two baking trays with baking paper or silicone baking mats.

Spread the walnuts over one of the baking trays and roast for 14–15 minutes or until fragrant and lightly golden. Allow them to cool completely before transferring to a food processor and blitzing into a fine meal.

Using an electric mixer fitted with the paddle attachment, mix the butter and caster sugar until pale and creamy, about 3–4 minutes. Add the egg, vanilla and salt and mix until combined, then add the ground walnuts and flour and mix until a soft dough forms.

Roll out the dough on a lightly floured bench until 6 mm (¼ inch) thick. Using a 5 cm (2 inch) cutter, cut the dough into rounds and place them on the baking trays.

Bake the cookies for 10–12 minutes or until lightly golden brown. Allow them to cool for 10 minutes on the trays before transferring to a wire rack to cool completely.

Spoon 1 teaspoon of the plum jam into the centre of half of the cookies and sandwich with the remaining cookies. Liberally dust with icing sugar.

Speculoos cream stars

Makes 30

Speculoos are a beautiful Belgian cookie that is subtly spiced, traditionally with cinnamon at the forefront, and flavoured with the toasty, treacly notes of brown sugar. You may also have seen them called speculaas; this spelling is for their Dutch counterpart. They are fragrant and crunchy and make the perfect base for a sandwich cookie filled with a cinnamon buttercream. While speculoos are traditionally baked using a decorative mould, because these are sandwiched I've cut them out with a star cutter. You can cut them into any shape you love.

You can make the cookie dough a day or two ahead and store it in the fridge until you're ready to roll it out.

100 g (3½ oz) unsalted
   butter, softened
300 g (10½ oz) brown sugar
2 eggs
1 tablespoon vanilla bean
   paste
1 teaspoon ground cinnamon
1 teaspoon ground ginger
1 teaspoon ground
   cardamon
½ teaspoon ground cloves
½ teaspoon ground nutmeg
½ teaspoon salt
½ teaspoon bicarbonate
   of soda (baking soda)
270 g (9½ oz) plain
   (all-purpose) flour
80 g (2¾ oz) almond meal

Cinnamon buttercream
100 g (3½ oz) unsalted
   butter, softened
200 g (7 oz) icing
   (confectioners') sugar
1 teaspoon ground cinnamon
1 tablespoon vanilla bean
   paste

Using an electric mixer fitted with the paddle attachment, mix the butter, brown sugar and eggs until smooth. Add the vanilla, spices, salt and bicarbonate of soda and mix until just combined. Add the flour and almond meal and beat for 5–6 minutes. This will make the soft dough easier to roll and shape.

Wrap the dough in plastic wrap and refrigerate for 1–2 hours or until firm. This can be made a couple of days in advance.

Preheat the oven to 160°C (315°F) fan-forced. Line two baking trays with baking paper or silicone baking mats.

Roll out the dough on a lightly floured bench until 3 mm (⅛ inch) thick. Use a 5 cm (2 inch) star cutter to cut out the cookies and place them on the baking trays.

Bake the cookies for 12–14 minutes or until they are deeply caramelised and golden. Allow them to cool for 10 minutes on the trays before transferring to a wire rack to cool completely.

For the cinnamon buttercream, use an electric mixer fitted with the paddle attachment to mix the butter, icing sugar, cinnamon and vanilla on medium speed for 6–8 minutes or until light and creamy.

Transfer the buttercream to a piping bag and snip off the end to make a 2 mm (1⁄16 inch) opening. Pipe a generous swirl of buttercream onto the centre of half the cookies, then sandwich with the remaining cookies.

Double-chocolate peppermint cookies

Makes 20

These cookies are Christmas, wrapped in a neat little bow. I'm fairly partial to the chocolate + mint combo, even more partial to Christmas peppermint bark and even more partial to a double-chocolate-chip cookie. Put it all together and you get these festive beauties.

180 g (6 oz) unsalted butter, softened
110 g (3¾ oz) brown sugar
125 g (4½ oz) caster (superfine) sugar
1 egg
1 teaspoon vanilla extract
½ teaspoon salt
190 g (6¾ oz) plain (all-purpose) flour
65 g (2¼ oz) dark cocoa powder
1 teaspoon bicarbonate of soda (baking soda)
200 g (7 oz) dark chocolate chips
100 g (3½ oz) white chocolate chips
4 large (about 60 g/2¼ oz) candy canes, chopped into small pieces

Garnish
100 g (3½ oz) white chocolate, melted
5 large candy canes, crushed

Preheat the oven to 160°C (315°F) fan-forced. Line two baking trays with baking paper or silicone baking mats.

Using an electric mixer fitted with the paddle attachment, cream the butter, brown sugar, caster sugar and egg until creamy and pale in colour. Add the vanilla and salt and mix to combine.

In a separate bowl, combine the flour, cocoa and bicarbonate of soda and whisk to combine.

Add the flour mixture to the butter mixture and mix on low speed until just combined, then add all of the chocolate chips and the chopped candy canes and mix to combine.

Divide the dough into balls, using 50 g (1¾ oz) dough for each one, and place them on the baking trays, leaving plenty of room for spreading.

Bake the cookies for 14–15 minutes or until puffy and set in the middle. To get your cookies perfectly round, see my tips on page 12. Allow them to cool for 10 minutes on the trays before transferring to a wire rack to cool completely.

For the garnish, spoon the melted white chocolate into a piping bag and snip off a small tip. Pipe the chocolate back and forth over the cookies, then sprinkle the crushed candy canes over the top before the chocolate sets. Allow the chocolate to set completely before eating or gifting.

Glazed gingerbread

Makes 24

I love glazed gingerbread. This one has a beautiful heat from the ginger and peppercorns, and is finished with a luscious vanilla glaze. Christmas perfection. Depending on how long you bake it, you could enjoy it soft and chewy, or firm enough to build your gingerbread house (sans glaze, of course!).

120 g (4¼ oz) unsalted
  butter, softened
150 g (5½ oz) brown sugar
1 egg
150 g (5½ oz) molasses
1 tablespoon ground
  ginger
1 tablespoon ground
  cinnamon
1 teaspoon ground cloves
¾ teaspoon ground pink
  peppercorns
½ teaspoon salt
480 g (1 lb 1 oz) plain
  (all-purpose) flour,
  plus extra for dusting
1 teaspoon baking powder
½ teaspoon bicarbonate
  of soda (baking soda)

Vanilla glaze
150 g (5½ oz) icing
  (confectioners') sugar
20 g (¾ oz) unsalted
  butter, melted
2–3 tablespoons milk
1 teaspoon vanilla bean
  paste

Using an electric mixer fitted with the paddle attachment, cream the butter, brown sugar and egg until light and fluffy, about 3–4 minutes. Add the molasses, spices and salt and mix until thoroughly combined. Add the flour, baking powder and bicarbonate of soda and mix on low speed until a soft dough forms.

Wrap the dough in plastic wrap and refrigerate for 2–3 hours or until firm to the touch.

Preheat the oven to 170°C (325°F) fan-forced. Line two baking trays with baking paper or silicone baking mats.

Roll out the dough on a lightly floured bench until 1 cm (½ inch) thick. Cut the gingerbread into shapes – I've used a decorative cookie press and tree cutter on these, but a simple gingerbread cutter will also be perfect. Place the gingerbread shapes on the baking trays.

Bake the gingerbread for 12–15 minutes or until it appears puffy and lightly golden. Allow the gingerbread to cool on the trays while you make the glaze.

For the glaze, simply combine all the icing sugar, melted butter and milk in a bowl and mix until smooth.

Use a pastry brush to brush the glaze over the surface of the cooled gingerbread. Allow the glaze to set completely before eating – around 1–2 hours at room temperature will do it.

Fruity meringue clouds

Makes 10
Gluten free

I know, these aren't technically cookies, but I've included them here in the festive-flavoured section of the book for a couple of reasons. Firstly, they make a beautiful, individual alternative to your Christmas pavlova. Secondly, they're just perfect for Christmas gifting. Most importantly, though, these meringue clouds are every child's Christmas wishes come true: big, colourful and full of punchy fruity flavour. Pictured here are meringues topped with a raspberry, blueberry and passionfruit reduction. You could also use mango, blackberry, strawberry or even cherry.

8 egg whites
400 g (14 oz) caster
   (superfine) sugar
1 tablespoon white vinegar
20 g (¾ oz) freeze-dried
   raspberry, blueberry
   or passionfruit powder
   (optional)

Fruit reduction
300 g (10½ oz) frozen
   raspberries, blueberries
   or passionfruit pulp
100 g (3½ oz) caster
   (superfine) sugar
⅛ teaspoon citric acid
   (optional)

For the fruit reduction, combine one type of fruit in a saucepan with 100 g (3½ oz) sugar and bring to the boil over medium heat. Continue to boil until the fruit has reduced by half to a sticky, syrupy consistency. Strain out any seeds and taste the mixture. If you'd like more tartness, mix in the citric acid. Allow the reduction to cool completely.

Preheat the oven to 90°C (195°F) fan-forced. Line two baking trays with baking paper or silicone baking mats.

Using an electric mixer fitted with the whisk attachment, mix the egg whites on medium speed until soft peaks begin to form. Slowly rain in the sugar while mixing. Once all of the sugar has been added, increase the speed to high and mix for 4–5 minutes or until the sugar has mostly dissolved and the meringue is thick and glossy. Mix in the vinegar.

Using a large kitchen spoon, spoon quenelles of the meringue directly onto the baking trays. Bake the meringues for 1 hour, then remove from the oven and brush the top of each meringue with 1–2 teaspoons of the fruit reduction. Return the meringues to the oven for a further 45 minutes. Turn off the oven and allow the meringues to cool completely in there – overnight is best.

Liberally dust the meringues with the freeze-dried fruit powder, if using. This is best done on the day you want to serve them.

Almond toffee bark

Makes 20 pieces
Gluten free

70 g (2½ oz) honey
150 g (5½ oz) caster
　(superfine) sugar
125 g (4½ oz) unsalted
　butter
200 g (7 oz) slivered
　almonds
250 g (9 oz) milk or dark
　chocolate, melted
Sea salt flakes

Here's another recipe that's more of a confection than a cookie. I just had to include this bark as it makes the most perfect gift. Mix it up by replacing the almonds with macadamias, peanuts, hazelnuts or pistachios. This recipe is all about trusting the process – it might look like it's not going to work, but it will! If you love Daim chocolate, you're in for a treat.

Line a baking tray with baking paper or a silicone baking mat.

Combine the honey, sugar and 1 tablespoon water in a saucepan over high heat. Add the butter and bring to the boil, stirring constantly, then keep stirring until the mixture reaches 150°C (302°F) on a sugar thermometer. Add the almonds and keep stirring until the thermometer reads 175–180°C (347–356°F), then remove from the heat.

Spread the mixture onto the baking tray and allow it to set for 10–15 minutes before scoring it with a knife. This will enable you to easily break it up once it sets. Allow the bark to set completely at room temperature.

Cover one side of the toffee slab with the melted chocolate and sprinkle with the sea salt. Once the chocolate has set, break the bark into pieces along the scored lines.

Vaniljekranse

Makes 25

Forgive me if this memory is specific to my childhood, but I have a feeling many of us can relate to this one... opening up your grandma's pantry and finding a big blue tin full of delicious buttery shortbreads sitting in their own little patty pans. Enter the Danish butter cookie, traditionally known as vaniljekranse, which directly translates to 'vanilla wreath'. The trick to making these a little easier to pipe is to start with really soft butter. If you don't, I predict a few burst piping bags in your future.

125 g (4½ oz) unsalted butter, softened
55 g (2 oz) icing (confectioners') sugar
2½ teaspoons vanilla bean paste
130 g (4½ oz) plain (all-purpose) flour
25 g (1 oz) cornflour (cornstarch)
75 g (2½ oz) caster (superfine) sugar, to garnish

Line two baking trays with baking paper or silicone baking mats.

Using an electric mixer fitted with the paddle attachment, mix the butter, icing sugar and vanilla on medium speed until pale and creamy, being sure to scrape down the side of the bowl a few times to ensure all of the butter is properly incorporated. Add the flour and cornflour and mix until a smooth paste forms. You want the dough to be quite soft to make it easy to pipe.

Transfer the dough to a piping bag fitted with a Wilton #1M star nozzle. Pipe little wreaths, approximately 4 cm (1½ inches) in diameter, onto the baking trays. Place the trays in the fridge for 2–4 hours (they can also be refrigerated overnight) to reduce spreading when the cookies are baking. You can also freeze the wreaths at this stage and bake as needed.

Preheat the oven to 170°C (325°F) fan-forced.

Bake the cookies for 18–20 minutes or until they begin to turn golden brown around the edges. While the cookies are still warm, sprinkle them with the caster sugar. Allow them to cool completely on the trays before packaging them up to gift.

Acknowledgements.

Craig, no words are needed but I know they're always appreciated. Our life is relentless at the moment, but I wouldn't change it for the world. Life with you is just magic – regimented and orderly, yet somehow chaotic magic.

Mum and Dad, I said it in the last book and I'll say it again: thank you for everything. Always believing in me, always championing me, always boasting about me. Thank you for caring for my babies so I could get this book done! Thank you for being my greatest allies.

My babies, Addie and Mac: Mama loves you more than she loves sugar and butter. You two are my entire purpose in life.

To my sister and my girlfriends, the inspiration for this book! There is a little bit of each of you in every one of these recipes and stories.

My Murdoch family, I would never want to do this with anyone other than you all. Your trust in me, your guidance in the process, your vision and execution, your ability to create everything I ever dreamed of in a book and more... I am absolutely honoured to call myself a Murdoch author.

Lee and Armelle, working with you both over the last couple of years has been an absolute highlight for me. Thank you for always knowing how to bring my books to life. You are integral to the story and I so appreciate you both.

Zahara, my dream gal. Working with you is flawless. Your pastry skills are perfection and I'm so lucky to call you a friend.

Genene, thank you for your recipe testing and shoot-baking prowess! There was a minute there when I thought this book was going to get the better of me, and you truly helped me see it to the finish.

Lena, thank you for everything you do for me beyond your impeccable management: namely, calming me down when I have my weekly toddler/baby breakdowns, for reminding me that I will find my way back to myself one day soon (that day will no doubt coincide with a full night's sleep) and listening to my endless, mindless, frustrated rants (you always seem to know when to call). Your support of my career is paramount to my success.

Finally, thank you to everyone out there who bought a copy of my first book and who has been so vocally excited for this book. Thank you for championing me. I'm very #blessed.

Index.

A

almonds
Almond and coconut chocolate clusters 180
Almond toffee bark 222
Bounty™ macarons 154-5
German pfeffernüsse 198-9
German poppy-seed and marzipan cookies 210
Macaroons (not to be confused with macarons) 39
Mango and green tea macarons 158-9
marzipan 210
Persian love cookies 182
Raspberry parfait macaron sandwiches 162-3
Seed and nut cookies 175
Speculoos cream stars 215
American buttercream 179
Anzac biscuits 52-3
Apple pie cookies 94
apricots
Apricot pistachio crumble bars 169
Rugelach 196

B

baking powder 16
Baklava cookies 104-5
bar cookies 10
Apricot pistachio crumble bars 169
chocolate-chip and pretzel cookie bars 62
Earl Grey millionaire shortbread 143-4
Lemon, lime and bitters bars 130
Limoncello spritz bars 170
matcha, white chocolate and raspberry cookie bars 62
Pecan pie shortbread bars 102
Raspberry rhubarb crumble bars 124
Strawberry and cream bar cookies 108
Triple-chocolate cookie bars 62
berries see blackberries; blueberries; currants; raspberries; strawberries
bicarbonate of soda 16
biscotti, Cinnamon, coffee and macadamia 166
Black Forest brookies 138
blackberries
blackberry and pink peppercorn kisses 85
Blackberry cheesecake cookies 123

blueberries
blueberry, lemon and white chocolate cookies 31
Blueberry muffin top cookies 110
Fruity meringue clouds 221
Bounty™ macarons 154-5
Brown butter, spiced oat and chocolate-chip cookies 58
Brown sugar and brown butter vanilla sables 43-4
brownies
Black Forest brookies 138
Buckwheat chocolate brownie cookies 48
Buckwheat chocolate brownie cookies 48
butter 15
buttercream
American buttercream 179
cinnamon buttercream 215
golden syrup buttercream 129
maple buttercream 136
white chocolate raspberry buttercream 51

C

caramel
caramel filling 97-8, 143
caramel pecan filling 102
Earl Grey millionaire shortbread 143-4
Pecan pie shortbread bars 102
Twixie Twix™ 97-8
Cashew kourabiedes 193
cereal chocolate-chip cookies 31
Chai-spiced sugar cookies 176
chantilly, chocolate 138
cheese see cream cheese; mascarpone
cheesecake cookies, Blackberry 123
cherries
Black Forest brookies 138
cherry compote 138
sour cherry and pistachio shortbread 27
white chocolate, sour cherry and pistachio cookies 31
Chewy ginger molasses cookies 34
chocolate 17
melting 17
tempering 17
see also chocolate, dark; chocolate, milk; chocolate, ruby; chocolate, white; cocoa
chocolate, dark
Almond and coconut chocolate clusters 180
Almond toffee bark 222
Black Forest brookies 138

blackberry and pink peppercorn kisses 85
Brown butter, spiced oat and chocolate-chip cookies 58
Buckwheat chocolate brownie cookies 48
cereal chocolate-chip cookies 31
chocolate chantilly 138
chocolate glaze 143-4
Chocolate marshmallow kisses 84-5
Chocolate wheaties 74
chocolate-chip and pretzel cookie bars 62
Chunky Levain-style malted chocolate-chip cookies 82
Cinnamon, coffee and macadamia biscotti 166
Cocoa meringue kisses 36
dark chocolate macadamia shortbread 27
Double-chocolate peppermint cookies 216
Earl Grey millionaire shortbread 143-4
Hazelnut praline squiggles 116-17
hazelnut-stuffed chocolate-chip cookies 31
milk chocolate hazelnut crunch cookies 31
Mint Slice™ biscuits, three ways 90-1
Miso dark chocolate flourless cookies 146
Passionfruit and chocolate sandwiches 152
passionfruit ganache 152
Pistachio and dark chocolate-chip cookies 141
Praline-stuffed chocolate-chip skillet cookie 80
Puerto Rican Besitos de Coco 209
Sables Korova 70
The only chocolate-chip cookie recipe you'll ever need 30-1
Triple-chocolate cookie bars 62
Viennese whirls 68
chocolate, milk
Almond toffee bark 222
Bounty™ macarons 154-5
chocolate coconut ganache 154
chocolate ganache 64
Chocolate hazelnut sandwiches 64
Chocolate marshmallow kisses 84-5
chocolate-dipped coffee shortbread 27
Chunky Levain-style malted chocolate-chip cookies 82
Hazelnut praline squiggles 116-17
Kingston™ biscuits 172

milk chocolate hazelnut crunch
cookies 31
strawberry milk chocolate kisses 85
Triple-chocolate cookie bars 62
Twixie Twix™ 97–8
chocolate, ruby: raspberry and ruby
chocolate cookies 31
chocolate, white
Blackberry cheesecake cookies 123
blueberry, lemon and white chocolate
cookies 31
Chai-spiced sugar cookies 176
Double-chocolate peppermint
cookies 216
dulcey passionfruit kisses 85
Hazelnut praline squiggles 116–17
Mango and green tea
macarons 158–9
mango ganache 158
matcha, white chocolate and
raspberry cookie bars 62
Matcha, white chocolate and
raspberry cookies 101
Pandan and coconut cookies 126
Raspberry and white chocolate
cornflake cookies 120
Raspberry white chocolate melting
moments 51
Seed and nut cookies 175
Strawberry and cream bar
cookies 108
Triple-chocolate cookie bars 62
white chocolate raspberry
buttercream 51
white chocolate, sour cherry
and pistachio cookies 31
Chunky Levain-style malted
chocolate-chip cookies 82
cinnamon
Baklava cookies 104–5
Chai-spiced sugar cookies 176
cinnamon buttercream 215
Cinnamon, coffee and macadamia
biscotti 166
French cinnamon palmiers 204
German pfeffernüsse 198–9
Glazed gingerbread 218
Speculoos cream stars 215
spiced syrup 105
citric acid 17
clusters, Almond and coconut
chocolate 180
cocoa 16
Bounty™ macarons 154–5
Chocolate ripples 73
Cocoa meringue kisses 36
Cookimisu 113
Double-chocolate peppermint
cookies 216

Mint Slice™ biscuits, three
ways 90–1
Miso dark chocolate flourless
cookies 146
Nutella melting moments 51
Passionfruit and chocolate
sandwiches 152
Sables Korova 70
Triple-chocolate cookie bars 62
see also chocolate
coconut
Almond and coconut chocolate
clusters 180
Anzac biscuits 52–3
Bounty™ macarons 154–5
chocolate coconut ganache 154
Chocolate wheaties 74
Iced VoVo™ biscuits 88
Kingston™ biscuits 172
lemon coconut shortbread 170
Limoncello spritz bars 170
Monte Carlo™ biscuits 179
Pandan and coconut cookies 126
Puerto Rican Besitos de Coco 209
Raspberry and white chocolate
cornflake cookies 120
coffee
chocolate-dipped coffee
shortbread 27
Cinnamon, coffee and macadamia
biscotti 166
Cookimisu 113
compote, cherry 138
cookies 10–11
baking and storing 21
how to get perfectly round 12
Cookimisu 113
cornflakes
Cereal chocolate-chip cookies 31
Raspberry and white chocolate
cornflake cookies 120
cream 16
cream cheese
Blackberry cheesecake cookies 123
Polish kolaczki 203
Rugelach 196
creams
chocolate chantilly 138
orange cream 149
see also buttercream
crinkle cookies, Lemon and poppy-
seed 67
crostoli, Italian 194
crumble topping 94, 110, 124
curds
curd topping 130
passionfruit curd 150
currants: Rugelach 196

D
dark chocolate *see* chocolate, dark
dates: Sticky date whoopie pies 129
Double-chocolate peppermint
cookies 216
drop cookies 10
dulcey passionfruit kisses 85

E
Earl Grey Anzac ice-cream
sandwiches 53
Earl Grey millionaire shortbread
143–4
eggs 15
Cocoa meringue kisses 36
curd topping 130
Fruity meringue clouds 221
passionfruit curd 150
raspberry parfait 162
equipment 18–19

F
filled cookies 10
flour 15
flourless cookies, Miso dark
chocolate 146
French cinnamon palmiers 204
Fruity meringue clouds 221

G
ganache
chocolate coconut ganache 154
chocolate ganache 64
mango ganache 158
passionfruit ganache 152
gelatine 17
German pfeffernüsse 198–9
German poppy-seed and marzipan
cookies 210
ginger
Chai-spiced sugar cookies 176
Chewy ginger molasses cookies 34
German pfeffernüsse 198–9
gingernut cookies 34
Glazed gingerbread 218
Speculoos cream stars 215
gingerbread, Glazed 218
Glazed gingerbread 218
gluten free
Almond and coconut chocolate
clusters 180
Almond toffee bark 222
Black Forest brookies 138
Bounty™ macarons 154–5
Buckwheat chocolate brownie
cookies 48
Cocoa meringue kisses 36
Fruity meringue clouds 221

Macaroons (not to be confused with macarons) 39
Mango and green tea macarons 158-9
Miso dark chocolate flourless cookies 146
Persian love cookies 182
Raspberry parfait macaron sandwiches 162-3
Seed and nut cookies 175
golden syrup buttercream 129

H

hazelnuts
Chocolate hazelnut sandwiches 64
Chunky Levain-style malted chocolate-chip cookies 82
hazelnut praline paste 116
Hazelnut praline squiggles 116-17
hazelnut-stuffed chocolate-chip cookies 31
Jammy thumbprints 46
milk chocolate hazelnut crunch cookies 31
Nutella melting moments 51
Praline-stuffed chocolate-chip skillet cookie 80
Spiced plum and hazelnut Linzer cookies 188
honey cookies, Sesame 61

I

ice-cream sandwiches, Earl Grey Anzac 53
Iced VoVo™ biscuits 88
icing, limoncello 170
ingredients 15-17
Italian crostoli 194

J

Jammy thumbprints 46

K

Kingston™ biscuits 172
Koulourakia, Mahlepi 190
kourabiedes, Cashew 193

L

Lady fingers 56
lebkuchengewürz 198
lemons
Blackberry cheesecake cookies 123
blueberry, lemon and white chocolate cookies 31
Blueberry muffin top cookies 110
curd topping 130
Italian crostoli 194
Lemon and poppy-seed crinkle cookies 67

lemon coconut shortbread 170
Lemon, lime and bitters bars 130
Limoncello spritz bars 170
limes
curd topping 130
Lemon, lime and bitters bars 130
limoncello icing 170
Limoncello spritz bars 170
Linzer cookies, Spiced plum and hazelnut 188

M

macadamias
Cinnamon, coffee and macadamia biscotti 166
dark chocolate macadamia shortbread 27
Passionfruit curd macadamia thumbprints 150
macarons
Bounty™ macarons 154-5
Mango and green tea macarons 158-9
Raspberry parfait macaron sandwiches 162-3
storing 21
Macaroons (not to be confused with macarons) 39
Mahlepi Koulourakia 190
malted milk powder: Chunky Levain-style malted chocolate-chip cookies 82
mangoes
Mango and green tea macarons 158-9
mango ganache 158
maple buttercream 136
Maple shortbread leaves 136
marshmallows
blackberry and pink peppercorn kisses 85
cereal chocolate-chip cookies 31
Chocolate marshmallow kisses 84-5
dulcey passionfruit kisses 85
strawberry milk chocolate kisses 85
vanilla marshmallow 84
marzipan
German poppy-seed and marzipan cookies 210
marzipan 210
mascarpone: Cookimisu 113
matcha
Mango and green tea macarons 158-9
matcha, white chocolate and raspberry cookie bars 62
Matcha, white chocolate and raspberry cookies 101

melting moments
Nutella melting moments 51
Raspberry white chocolate melting moments 51
meringues
Cocoa meringue kisses 36
Fruity meringue clouds 221
milk chocolate see chocolate, milk
Mint Slice™ biscuits, three ways 90-1
Miso dark chocolate flourless cookies 146
Monte Carlo™ biscuits 179
moulded cookies 11
muffin top cookies, Blueberry 110

N

no-bake cookies 11
Nutella melting moments 51
nuts and nut meals 16
see also almonds; cashews; hazelnuts; macadamias; peanuts; pecans; pistachios; walnuts

O

oats
Anzac biscuits 52-3
Brown butter, spiced oat and chocolate-chip cookies 58
Kingston™ biscuits 172
oranges
Baklava cookies 104-5
Jammy thumbprints 46
Macaroons (not to be confused with macarons) 39
Mahlepi Koulourakia 190
orange cream 149
Orange creams 149
spiced syrup 105
Viennese whirls 68

P

palmiers, French cinnamon 204
Pandan and coconut cookies 126
parfait, raspberry 162
passionfruit
dulcey passionfruit kisses 85
Fruity meringue clouds 221
Mint Slice™ biscuits, three ways 90-1
Passionfruit and chocolate sandwiches 152
passionfruit curd 150
Passionfruit curd macadamia thumbprints 150
passionfruit ganache 152
peanuts: The peanut butter cookie that almost wasn't 40

Emelia Jackson loves to make people happy through butter and sugar. A sought-after cake designer and recipe creator, she is the author of bestselling modern baking bible *First, Cream the Butter and Sugar* – a book that has inspired dozens of fans to bake their way through all 150 perfect recipes. Emelia rose to prominence when she was victorious in the 2020 Australian MasterChef *Back to Win* series, where she displayed her razor-sharp focus on the perfect cake and pastry. The only thing Emelia loves more than choux pastry is a basic cookie.